CW01239370

Seven Myths About Money

Also by Rob Dix

The Price of Money

The Complete Guide to Property Investment

Seven Myths About Money

And the Truth About Finding Financial Freedom

ROB DIX

Cornerstone Press

CORNERSTONE PRESS

UK | USA | Canada | Ireland | Australia
India | New Zealand | South Africa

Cornerstone Press is part of the Penguin Random House group of companies whose addresses can be found at global.penguinrandomhouse.com

Penguin Random House UK,
One Embassy Gardens, 8 Viaduct Gardens, London SW11 7BW

penguin.co.uk
global.penguinrandomhouse.com

Penguin Random House UK

First published 2025
001

Copyright © Rob Dix, 2025

The moral right of the author has been asserted

Penguin Random House values and supports copyright. Copyright fuels creativity, encourages diverse voices, promotes freedom of expression and supports a vibrant culture. Thank you for purchasing an authorised edition of this book and for respecting intellectual property laws by not reproducing, scanning or distributing any part of it by any means without permission. You are supporting authors and enabling Penguin Random House to continue to publish books for everyone. No part of this book may be used or reproduced in any manner for the purpose of training artificial intelligence technologies or systems. In accordance with Article 4(3) of the DSM Directive 2019/790, Penguin Random House expressly reserves this work from the text and data mining exception.

Typeset in 11.6/14.75pt Dante MT Std by Jouve (UK), Milton Keynes
Printed and bound in Great Britain by Clays Ltd, Elcograf S.p.A.

The authorised representative in the EEA is Penguin Random House Ireland, Morrison Chambers, 32 Nassau Street, Dublin D02 YH68

A CIP catalogue record for this book is available from the British Library

ISBN: 978–1–529–91096–4

Penguin Random House is committed to a sustainable future for our business, our readers and our planet. This book is made from Forest Stewardship Council® certified paper.

CONTENTS

Introduction: New Game, New Rules   3

1. The Saving Myth   17

2. The Early Retirement Myth   39

3. The Risk-Minimisation Myth   63

4. The Home-Ownership Myth   79

5. The Compounding Myth   97

6. The Diversification Myth   115

7. The 'Too Risky' Myth   137

Conclusion: A Myth-Buster's Guide to Financial Freedom   155

Notes   175

Index   187

About the Author   193

Seven Myths About Money

INTRODUCTION What if everything you've been told about money is wrong?

INTRODUCTION
NEW GAME, NEW RULES

It might not always feel like it, but you're lucky enough to be living through the best period in human history.

From the evolution of the first modern humans 300,000 years ago until literally the last few centuries, mere survival was considered an A+ result. If you managed to work brutally hard every day from childhood until you died of old age – without famine, rampant disease or war wiping you out before you got there – you'd have been one of the world's winners. If you were outlived by more than half of your children, you'd have lived a charmed life indeed.

Fast forward to today and life is better than ever in just about every way. You're less likely to die of disease, as illnesses that once would have been a death sentence are now treatable. You own a magical device that can instantaneously distract you with the world's accumulated knowledge, and allow you to maintain relationships with friends all over the world. You might be listening to this book on a wireless speaker that's nestled in your ear or reading it as you're whisked in (relative) comfort across great distances.

Yet there's one area in which life *isn't* better for the average person than ever before: money.

If you'd graduated high school in the 1960s, you could have walked straight into a professional career, with no university degree and resultant student debt required. A single earner could support a typical family, and by saving up four years' salary you could buy a typical home. You would have gone on to live through a period where any assets you owned – including your home – rocketed in value. And, as if that weren't enough, you might have retired with a pension linked to your final salary – regardless of how well financial markets had performed. Merely by following the herd from school to workplace and copying the financial habits of your peers, it was possible to live a comfortable financial life.

Not any more. By following the default choices now, you might find yourself at university – driven not by a deep desire to learn, but because it's the only way into most jobs – and then leave with debt that it takes most of your working life to pay off. You then find that you need two salaries to support your family, and you can't afford to buy a home until you're well into your thirties.

If you want to retire in comfort, then you need to save hard to make investments (while also saving to buy that expensive house) and cross your fingers. If you're not able to retire, at least you won't be alone: at the time of writing, the number of over seventies in the workforce in the UK has increased by 61 per cent over the past ten years, and in the US it's expected to grow by another 96 per cent in the next five years. Across Europe, the share of workers aged fifty-five years or older increased from 12 per cent to 20 per cent between 2004 and 2019.

Yes, your life will still be better than those of your ancestors by many metrics – but money touches all the metrics that are left over. If you're doing worse financially, it's going to hurt.

THE YEAR THAT CHANGED EVERYTHING

Why are things so different now from half a century ago? The beginnings of our answer can be found on one of my favourite websites: wtfhappenedin1971.com.

Started as a joke by a couple of anonymous social media

accounts, 'WTF happened in 1971?' collates graphs and charts pointing to a surprisingly widespread set of financial and social changes that started in the early 1970s. Now, though, the collection has grown to a point where it's not funny – and is actually rather disturbing.

It shows that, up until 1971, productivity growth and worker compensation moved in line with each other in most of the rich world – suggesting that people were benefiting from the gains generated by new technology and more efficient working practices. From then onwards, productivity continued to grow. But wages stagnated: the gains were going elsewhere.

It also shows that inequality – as measured by the gap between the richest 5 per cent and the bottom 20 per cent – had been roughly the same for decades. Until 1971, that is. After that point a yawning chasm began to open: the richest got richer and everyone else was left further behind.

Across a startling array of measures – from savings rates to the number of working hours required to buy a house, and even divorce and incarceration rates – you can look at dozens of charts and see a consistent trendline up until the 1970s, at which point it suddenly changes course (usually for the worse). What, indeed, TF happened?

Well, 1971 wasn't just picked at random. In fact, it was the year when the system that had underpinned the global economy since the end of the Second World War – the gold standard – came to an end.

As the name suggests, under this system the value of the world's major currencies was defined in relation to gold: every US dollar could be converted into a fixed amount of gold by foreign governments, and many other currencies were pegged to the dollar at a fixed rate of exchange. The result? Without getting its hands on more shiny metal to cover any demands to turn dollars into gold, the Federal Reserve (the central bank of the US) was limited in its ability to increase the supply of dollars in circulation.

When this system was abruptly scrapped by President Nixon one Sunday evening in August, a new financial era began. The world's major currencies were now untethered from anything, and had value purely because governments said they did. This gave central banks far more flexibility to manipulate the economy – because, suddenly, they could more strongly influence the amount of money in circulation, with all the knock-on effects that had on inflation, interest rates and productivity.

Economists disagree among themselves (as they disagree on virtually everything) as to how much of what's happened since has been the result of central banks wielding these powers unwisely, and how much is due to completely unrelated factors, like changing demographics, globalisation and investor behaviour. But what's indisputable is that, in the years after that fateful Sunday evening, the world economy would start moving in a very different direction – experiencing first spiralling inflation, then more sluggish productivity growth, and then, in the longer term, a startling downward drift in the rate of interest.

The long-term average for interest rates in the US and UK, going back as far as reliable data is available, is roughly 4–5 per cent. After rates hit historical all-time highs during the inflationary 1970s, they moved downwards throughout the 1980s and 1990s – eventually falling to levels below 2 per cent in the US by the early 2000s. Naturally, as money becomes ever-cheaper, it's rational to borrow more – which is what governments, corporations and individuals alike chose to do over these decades. Globally, the total level of debt to GDP practically doubled from just over 100 per cent in 1971 to 195 per cent by 2007.

In the wake of the 2007–2008 financial crisis, this longstanding trend would go into overdrive. A banking collapse that started with subprime loans in America triggered a loss of trust across the financial sector, and brought down supposedly 'too big to fail' institutions that had been around for hundreds of years. In the ensuing panic, central banks took full advantage of their powers and acted quickly to put the economy on life support – reducing the cost of borrowing even further to stimulate as much economic activity as possible, and flooding the system with unprecedented amounts of newly created money. Interest rates were slashed to previously unthinkable lows: in the US and UK, rates were set at just above zero, and in the Eurozone they even turned negative. And the cheaper debt became, the more that was borrowed. In the US, government debt (which had already doubled to 62 per cent of GDP by 2007) reached 97 per cent only a few years after the crisis, in 2012.

It's clear that during the forty years since the end of the gold standard ushered in a new financial era, the world had become hooked on cheap debt. For every crisis, the creation of ever-more, ever-cheaper debt was part of the solution – and in between crises, things seldom moved back in the opposite direction. Even by the beginning of 2020 – twelve years on from the 2007–2008 collapse – interest rates had barely crept above their all-time lows. Meanwhile, the combined global debt levels of governments, businesses and individuals exceeded 250 per cent of GDP, reaching a total of $226 trillion.

Many people benefited from this era of ever-higher, ever-cheaper debt. But not everyone. The winners were those with assets. Stocks, bonds and real estate all benefit from falling interest rates: borrowing becomes cheaper, leading to increased demand for assets, which drives their prices up. (In fact, they won twice over – because they could also borrow cheap money to get their hands on even more assets.) The losers were, well, everyone else – going some way to explaining that 'WTF' inequality gap.

But at least by the time the 'free money' era got into full swing in the years after 2007, it was obvious how to play the game. Buy the biggest home you can as soon as you can, because debt was so cheap it'd be silly not to. Invest in the stock and bond markets, because both were only going in one direction – meaning that without trying too hard or taking too much risk, a passive investor could enjoy double-digit annual returns. And, with inflation being so low, there was no need to worry too much about the bite it'd take out of your gains.

As long as conditions stayed the same, so would the rules of the game. Of course, if interest rates reversed course, then there'd be some consequences to face. But those days were gone for good, right?

THE END OF THE OLD ORDER

Wrong. It may not have been marked by a televised presidential announcement this time, but another new era has begun. The financial world that we've lived in for most or all of our lives has changed, potentially for ever – and this book is your guide to navigating it.

Starting in the early years of the 2020s, the forces that had defined the world's economy for half a century – and which stepped up several gears following the financial crisis – screeched to a halt and reversed, at a pace that took everyone by surprise. Inflation, which had been thought of as a problem of the past, returned with a vengeance. And suddenly, to combat it, interest rates rebounded from near-zero all the way back up to their long-term average. As we'll learn in the chapters that follow, while the worst inflationary pressures of the early 2020s may have subsided, it's hard to imagine interest rates falling back to the historic lows that defined the world of the last few decades – nor inflation being brought fully under control for good.

The easy money party is over – and the hangover that we're living through now could be a particularly painful one.

New Game, New Rules

For one thing, the embedded assumption that assets only rise in value has been shattered: the forces that pushed all asset prices upwards at the same time have abated, leaving us in for a far bumpier ride. For another, inflation will keep rearing up and threatening our living standards.

On top of that, governments are less able to help than ever before – and may even be coming cap-in-hand asking you to help them instead. After all, governments now find themselves in the same position as the homeowner who used cheap money to buy a house they couldn't otherwise afford: those trillions of dollars of debt will eventually need to be refinanced at higher rates, meaning that debt repayments will take up a larger share of tax revenue. Borrowing more money just to cover everyday commitments – as the US government has done in every year but four since 1971, and the UK government has done in every year but five – suddenly seems less appealing. The only way out is through cutbacks, tax increases and inflation.

So it doesn't take a crystal ball or an economics degree for the average person – who's already spent the past 50+ years falling further behind – to see that life is likely to get significantly worse.

But there is a way out. My belief – and the case I'll make throughout this book – is that it is possible to thrive in this new economic era. It just involves forgetting a large amount of what you've been told – and being prepared to bust a few myths.

The word 'myth' has several meanings. It can refer to a story passed down through the ages. It can mean a widely held but false idea. It can mean a deliberate misrepresentation of the truth, or an idealised picture of it. Today, most of what you hear about money – even if once true – has taken on at least one of these qualities. The old-school financial wisdom – much of which was already woefully out of date even by the turn of the twenty-first century – is now rooted in myth as much as in fact.

Seven Myths About Money

It's a myth, for example, that savings are always going to come to your rescue when times get tough (what happens if inflation is higher than the interest paid by your bank?). It's a myth that 'compounding returns' are all you need for a happy retirement (what happens when the rate of compounding is lower than the old models would ever have predicted?). And it's a myth that you should never try to beat the market (what if times are tough enough that doing so is the only way to get ahead?).

In this book I'll be tackling the seven biggest and most pernicious misconceptions, half-truths and outright lies about money head-on. And in debunking them, I'll sketch out an alternative route to financial independence – one that will help you thrive in the new reality of today's financial system.

Don't get me wrong: I'm not a finance 'natural' or any kind of guru. I've only come to discover this new path by trying out all the old advice, keeping the rare bits that succeeded, and filling the gaps with experiments inspired by some decidedly unconventional sources. For every one of my stranger money moves that worked – like posting banknotes to a stranger to buy Bitcoin before anyone beyond online weirdos had heard of it, or refusing to buy the home I live in despite presenting a show called *The Property Podcast* – I had two that didn't. (It turns out that reflexively buying cheap shares in a company because everyone thought it was about to go bankrupt was ill-advised: sometimes, the majority is right.)

But over the past fifteen years, I've studied the worlds of economics and personal finance intensively – questioning everything, and learning which ideas about money are correct and which are nothing more than hearsay. Over time this has developed into an alternative rulebook that has worked for me, and which I've seen work for a huge number of others too. If it worked for them, and it worked for me, it might just work for you too.

New Game, New Rules

MONEY RULES FOR THE REAL WORLD

Turning your back on conventional wisdom can be a little daunting – particularly when many of the misconceptions we'll explore in this book have been following you for your whole life. But if abandoning the myths of the past doesn't come naturally, don't worry: I won't be asking you to do anything extreme.

In fact, that's the first of four 'red lines' I put in place when I was designing this method for myself – and which are, for me, the basis of any sane approach to your finances. These guiding principles are clearly needed, because even when the world of money was a more straightforward place – and some of today's myths still qualified as sound advice – most people struggled to get ahead financially all the same. The problem wasn't a lack of knowledge; it was that much of what was being asked ran counter to human nature. You were being handed a plan that would have worked perfectly, provided you could suppress all your impulses for decades on end.

For me, a method only has value if what it preaches is something people are able to follow – and, ideally, are excited about following. That's how I came to set myself these four ground rules.

Red line 1: It doesn't require major life changes

Sure, most people on *The Sunday Times* Rich List got there by taking big entrepreneurial bets (if they didn't have the foresight to be born into wealth already). Many friends of mine found their way to wealth by moving to the other side of the world in search of new opportunities and a cheaper cost of living.

If you're wired to take risks and follow your own path, great – but for most of us it's not realistic, and nor is it necessary. In fact, following my method will make your financial life feel simpler and less risky than it is now.

Red line 2: It doesn't take decades to work

If I had a doctor who said she had a fool-proof plan for curing me but it'd take forty years, I'd go looking for a new doctor.

Personal finance books are full of great advice for what you can do in your early twenties to secure your eventual retirement. But what about those of us for whom that ship sailed long ago? Or what if you do have youth on your side, but you're not willing to wait that long?

Following my alternative prescription won't see you showered in instant riches – that's just not realistic. But you'll start to sense a difference within a year, be on a whole new financial trajectory after three to five years, and have radically transformed your life within a decade.

Red line 3: It doesn't require endlessly delayed gratification

There's a subculture of people called 'life extensionists' who abstain from alcohol, processed foods and sugar because they believe it will extend their lifespan – perhaps even keeping them going until advances in medical science manage to find a complete cure for ageing. The joke about this group goes that they may not live for ever, but it'll certainly feel that way.

The same goes for money: I don't think we should deprive ourselves completely today for the sake of a distant future (which, without wanting to be too morbid, we're not guaranteed to live to see). Yes, Future You is important, and we need to look out for them. But Present You deserves some love too, so my method is focused on providing for the future while also improving your life today.

New Game, New Rules

Red line 4: It doesn't rely on anyone else

If your financial plan relies on the stock market behaving a certain way, a boss agreeing to a promotion or the government adopting a particular policy, you don't have a plan at all – you have a wish list.

It's even highly risky to base a plan on the assumption that the world will continue to be the same as it has been in the past. If there's one thing the history of economics tells us, it's that circumstances are prone to suddenly and dramatically changing at precisely the moment that everyone has forgotten how to imagine an alternative. That's why the success of this method is based on your actions alone – and if the world changes, it gives you the confidence and mental flexibility to adapt accordingly.

After debunking all seven myths in turn, I'll share a full eight-step plan based on this new reality, and direct you towards some extra resources I've put together to ensure you can put your plan into action. Ultimately, you'll have a fresh blueprint to navigate a new world: one that will bring you the kind of success that will always evade you if you stick to the traditional approach.

And if we're going to become myth-busters, we may as well start by overturning the most firmly embedded of them all.

1

MYTH The path to wealth begins with a healthy balance in your savings account.

REALITY Today, saving money often means losing money. The true path to wealth involves setting up good habits, then focusing elsewhere.

CHAPTER 1
THE SAVING MYTH

Other than the references to correct telegraph etiquette and the complete absence of women, you could be forgiven for confusing self-help books from the 1920s with those of today. In fact, it's astonishing how little of the advice they offer has changed over a century: set goals, think positively, improve your social skills, look after your health.

Perhaps this shouldn't be so surprising: our outfits and social norms may have changed, but physically and mentally we're not so different from our great-great-grandparents. Adopting Charles Atlas's fitness programme will leave you just as buff as Crossfit will, and using someone's name – as Dale Carnegie's 1936 classic *How to Win Friends and Influence People* emphasised – will charm them every bit as much over WhatsApp as it did when leaving a calling card.

But in the realm of money and finance, it's a different story entirely. In the 1920s the Federal Reserve was only just coming into existence, personal tax rates in the US were as low as 4 per cent for the typical earner, and most people would work up until five to ten years before they died. As a result of these and countless other changes, personal finance advice from a century ago was intended for a completely different world.

The trouble is, the ideas we're encouraged to apply today have changed astonishingly little. Take saving. The classic book *The Richest Man in Babylon* by George S. Clason, first published in 1926, said: 'For every ten coins thou placest within thy purse take out for use but nine. Thy purse will start to fatten at once and its increasing weight will feel good in thy hand and bring satisfaction to thy soul' – which is an impressively wordy way of saying 'save 10 per cent'. Although it originated much earlier, this idea really came to dominate from the 1980s onwards. By the turn of the millennium, it was everywhere. The 2003 mega-bestseller *The Automatic Millionaire* by David Bach reinforced the target of 10 per cent, while later that year Dave Ramsey's *The Total Money Makeover* upgraded it to 15 per cent.

These books never claimed that savings alone would be enough – but they gave the strong impression that saving a reasonable amount and making straightforward, sensible investments would leave the average reader financially comfortable. Perhaps a couple of decades ago they were right. But, today, following this advice is likely to leave you unsatisfied. In fact, there's seldom been a worse time to be a saver.

SAVING MONEY MEANS LOSING MONEY

A near constant over the past century has been the existence of inflation. Every year, prices rise and the value of your money shrinks. However, for most of that time it hasn't caused too much of a problem.

This is because in the US and most other Western economies, from the post-war era until 2008 (except for a couple of brief interludes in the 1970s), the rate of interest you could expect to earn on your savings was higher than the rate of inflation. Result: your money bought a little less every year, but your bank account was topped up with extra money that more than made up for it.

Yet in an attempt to jump-start the global economy after the financial meltdown in 2007, interest rates dropped to almost zero: central bankers' way of encouraging people and businesses to spend and invest now, rather than save for later. This meant that even the tiniest bit of inflation ended up being higher than the rate of interest. As a result, money in the bank started losing value. Suddenly, savers were being punished – and they would continue taking this punishment for the next fifteen years.

At least, though, everyone could see this happening: when your bank is offering you 0 per cent interest yet your weekly groceries keep on getting more expensive, you notice. But, in 2022, something insidious happened. First, inflation picked up. The chaos wrought by the Covid-19 lockdowns led to huge trade disruptions – and to a wave of money-printing on the part of central banks desperate to stimulate the economy. When the lockdowns lifted, increased demand in a world awash with cash sent prices spiralling. In the UK and Eurozone, inflation reached double digits, and in the US it peaked at 9.1 per cent.

In response, central banks finally picked interest rates off the floor. Higher interest rates make it more expensive to borrow money. The theory goes that this should stop consumers spending so much because their mortgage and other debts will absorb a higher amount of their income. This should bring supply and demand back into balance, and stop prices from going up any further.

In a pattern shared across most major economies, interest rates went from close to nothing to more than 5 per cent in little over a year. This would be considered rapid in any historical context – but with rates having sat almost untouched for more than a decade, it amounted to a level of shock treatment unheard of for over fifty years.

At first glance, this seemed like good news for savers: previously accustomed to earning nothing in the bank, you might suddenly be paid an interest rate of 5 per cent. But there was a catch: although interest rates picked up, most of the time they were still lower than the rate of inflation. If you had started 2022 with £100 in the bank and ended it with £105, it would have felt, for the first time in almost a generation, like you were getting ahead. But if you took the money out and spent it, you would have found that it bought you less than when you put it in.

The interest rate minus the rate of inflation is known as the 'real' interest rate. The 'real' rate was negative for the whole period between 2008 and 2022: in other words, leaving money in the bank would leave you slipping further behind. Since interest rates started picking up in 2022, there have been interludes when it has turned positive (meaning savers come out ahead). And there are some economists who believe that's the world we're on track to return to.

But I'm not so sure. In fact, I'd argue that it's as good as guaranteed that savers will continue to be punished in the future, for a whole host of reasons.

For a start, it's the only way governments can control their debts. From the creation of the Federal Reserve in 1923 up until now, as I'm writing this book, successive US governments have run up a total debt of $33 trillion. That sounds like a scarily large number. But the truly scary part is this: $20 trillion of that debt – getting on for two-thirds – has been accumulated in the last fifteen years alone. This wasn't so much of a problem while global interest rates were falling. In 2001, the US was paying an average interest rate of 6.5 per cent on its debt; by 2020 this had fallen to 2.4 per cent. Just like a cheaper rate on your mortgage would allow you to buy a bigger house for the same monthly cost, the US (and most other advanced economies around the world) could borrow more money without the repayments taking up a larger share of their tax revenues. So they increased their spending, and let the trillions pile up. Between 2004 and 2024, US government debt grew almost fivefold – yet the economy barely doubled in size. Debt as a proportion of GDP rose from 55 per cent to 123 per cent.

The Saving Myth

That's not ideal: the government had borrowed a vast amount of money but hadn't grown the economy by nearly as much. But it was manageable for as long as the cost of that debt remained low. Yet from 2022 onwards that ceased to be the case: higher interest rates mean higher borrowing costs for everyone, including governments.

The 'free money' era went on for so long that it became the norm – and governments found themselves thoroughly reliant on cheap debt. Between 2022 and 2023 alone, US government debt increased by half a trillion dollars – not for any special 'nice to have' spending, but purely to keep the lights on. In common with other economies, like the UK and the Eurozone, they've committed to levels of spending that have left them with no choice but to keep borrowing more and more every year – even as the cost of the interest on that debt increases.

This is, of course, a vicious cycle: the higher the debt repayments, the more money they need to borrow purely to pay the interest on the debt. This leaves them with less money left over to fund their other commitments, so they need to borrow yet more to pay for those. Which results in higher repayments . . . and on it goes.

So what can governments do about this? Ultimately, not much: it's almost impossible to imagine a scenario where governments are able to raise taxes enough or cut costs enough to end up with a surplus that they can use to pay down their debts. It's scary to think that the public services you rely on are only made possible by borrowing more every year, and that a substantial proportion of your taxes goes towards paying the interest on debt that's already been borrowed and spent – but it's true. In fact, at the time of writing, 39 cents of every dollar of income tax paid in the US is being used purely to pay interest on the debt.

All they can do is attempt to control the situation, by keeping the cost of borrowing as low as possible. The most important factor in determining that is the benchmark rate of interest, which is set by the central bank and heavily impacts the cost of borrowing across the economy. This is known as the 'base rate' or 'bank rate' in the UK, and the 'Fed Funds rate' in the US. Of course, all major central banks are technically independent from government and everyone involved will swear up and down that there's no political interference. But . . . there totally is political interference. While future rates of interest will almost certainly be higher in the coming decade than they were in the abnormally low 2010s, it seems unlikely they'll ever be allowed to settle at the much higher levels that were considered 'normal' in the twentieth century.

At the same time, inflation looks likely to spend the next few decades causing far more of a problem than we've become used to. There are countless reasons for this. First, there's the fact that the mere existence of inflation in the recent past is itself inflationary: economists worry about an 'inflationary spiral', where people see their living costs rising and demand to be paid more, which fuels inflation still further. In 2022, the Governor of the Bank of England suggested that workers should exercise 'restraint' in asking for pay rises for precisely this reason. Economically speaking, he was spot on – but given that he earns eighteen times more than the average Brit, it didn't go down particularly well.

Then there's the increasing fragility of global supply chains. The Covid lockdowns were inflationary in large part because it became much more difficult to get the stuff we need from place to place. Now think of all the other factors that could cause this to happen again, from economic frictions in Europe to geopolitical tensions in the Middle East. The world economy is becoming more unstable – and businesses suddenly consider it safer to make more products close to home, even if that comes at a higher cost than doing so on the other side of the globe.

The Saving Myth

There's also the desire to move away from fossil fuels and towards greener, more renewable forms of energy. However urgent this may be, there's no getting away from the fact that these alternative energy sources aren't yet as efficient as the ones they're replacing. As a result, it will likely push up the cost of energy – and as energy is an input to everything, that's inflationary too.

And there's one more factor. While central banks are rightly fearful of spiking inflation and clamped down hard on the double-digit levels that much of the world suffered in the early 2020s, a moderately high level of inflation is actually rather useful to them. That's because it helps to handle the enormous debt pile that almost all governments have built up – and which were pushed to new highs during the Covid years. If the price of everything (including wages) goes up, it increases the total size of the economy (GDP): nothing more has been produced, but the nominal value of it is higher. As a result, while the absolute amount of debt has remained the same, debt as a proportion of GDP has fallen.

You'll notice that 'the price of everything goes up' is another way of saying 'inflation': in other words, governments want *some* inflation. And what the government wants, it tends to get.

I'm not suggesting that hyperinflation is imminent in the US, UK or anywhere else. That would be disastrous for governments' credibility and their ability to borrow cheaply. But, overall, the government is motivated to create conditions where interest rates are relatively low, and inflation is as high as people will tolerate. In fact, I'd wager that this will be the hallmark of the next few decades. Where the post-2008 era was defined by vanishingly low interest rates and minimal inflation, the 2020s will be defined by interest rates that are higher than we've become used to, yet not really as high as they should be – paired with higher and more volatile rates of inflation.

The likely result for savers? A rate of inflation that spends most of its time above the rate of interest, and money in your bank account that buys you less with every passing year.

HOW TO PUT SAVING ON AUTOPILOT

How should we respond to the deck being stacked against savers to a historically unprecedented degree? One option is to give up completely and live purely for today. Tempting though it may be, Future You deserves better than that – especially given that governments may need to make cutbacks to the support they offer if you fall upon hard times.

Unfortunately, the more mainstream (and less hedonistic) financial advice also doesn't work. If you just carry on saving, you'll be swimming against the tide: making ever greater sacrifices across all areas of your life without much to show for it. Yes, we should continue to save – but not in the expectation that it's going to change our lives, or even be sufficient on its own to secure our future. In other words, we should give saving as much attention as necessary but no more – then dedicate that freed-up focus to the other ideas we'll be exploring in this book.

My approach to saving goes back to the very essence of why we spend money in the first place. Whenever we spend, we're implicitly saying that we value the thing we're buying more than we value the money we're giving up in exchange. It might not always feel like it (nobody relishes paying their electricity bill), but as long as you're making spending decisions of your own volition it's always true (you'd rather spend the money than live in the dark).

In theory, then, every time we spend money we should experience an improvement in our quality of life: if we don't, we shouldn't have made the trade. But even though nobody is compelling you to make spending decisions against your will, you've

The Saving Myth

probably noticed that you often end up spending money in ways that don't improve your life.

- Maybe it seems like it will make you happier, but you regret it almost immediately.

- Maybe it made you happy once, but you don't enjoy that activity as much and haven't stopped to re-evaluate the decision.

- Maybe it makes other people happy and you assume it should make you happy too, but you haven't been honest with yourself about it.

- Maybe it started out as an occasional treat that you loved, but now it's become so routine that you don't get much fresh enjoyment from it.

- Maybe you're not using it any more and you forgot you were even still paying for it.

I've developed a six-step process that's designed to minimise these spending 'mistakes', and I call the end result *mindful spending*. When you spend mindfully, you can be confident that the answer to 'will spending this money truly make me happier?' is always a resounding 'yes'.

This is, if you ask me, a pretty neat way of having your cake and eating it. Because you're only cutting spending in areas you've consciously decided don't contribute to your happiness, this reduction in your outgoings improves your future while having no negative impact on the present whatsoever.

There's no chance you have perfectly optimal spending already, so there will always be something you can eliminate – allowing you to increase the amount you can save without trying too hard.

Ready to start spending mindfully? There are six steps to follow.

Seven Myths About Money

Step 1: Don't make a budget

Not bad – only six steps, and the first of them involves *not* doing something.

'Make a budget' is the first step of any article you ever read about personal finance, but I believe it has major drawbacks – and the mindful spending process renders it unnecessary.

A major limitation of budgeting is that your biggest expenses are fixed. For example, the UK's Office for National Statistics reports that housing, food, healthcare, insurance and transportation combined makes up 72 per cent of the average family's total expenditure. In the US, the Bureau of Labour Statistics calculates that the figure is closer to 82.5 per cent. So you can dither around wondering if you should allow yourself a £5 or £10 weekly coffee budget, but this discretionary spending makes up such a small fraction of your overall outgoings that you're only fiddling around the edges.

It's also a waste of brainpower. Unless you're one of those rare and slightly odd people for whom personal finance is a hobby, you have limited time and energy to devote to your finances.

Putting a budget together in the first place isn't the demanding part, and can even be weirdly rewarding: it imposes a theoretical order on your life and makes you feel like you're getting your act together. That's great – but then you need to actually stick to it. And constantly monitoring your adherence to a budget will suck up a valuable portion of the limited attention and willpower you're willing to invest into this area of your life. Your precious mental capacity is better spent on activities that will give you more bang for your cognitive buck – like earning more, and investing well.

There's also a risk that budgeting will become such a grind that you end up resenting the whole endeavour, and give up on improving your finances at all – which would be a shame, because

The Saving Myth

there are far more enjoyable and effective actions you could be taking.

Of course, it might be that you need the structure of a budget, or that you find it mentally helpful to have one: maybe it relaxes you rather than depresses you. It might be that you currently don't have a choice: you need a budget to make sure there's enough money to last you to the end of the month. If the idea of budgeting appeals to you for these or any other reasons, feel free to ignore this step. I'm just offering an alternative for the large number of people who find it a total downer.

Step 2: Track your everyday spending

This is my secret weapon for keeping spending consistently reasonable without going anywhere near a budget.

It works like this: every time you spend money, note it down. For maximum psychological impact, do it immediately afterwards rather than in a batch at the end of a day.

The way you record it doesn't matter: the notes app on your phone is perfectly good enough. If you want to, you can use an app that adds everything up for you and allows you to do some whizzy data analysis by category. The key part, though, is that you do it manually. Anything that connects automatically to your bank and keeps track of everything for you won't do the job.

Whenever you spend any amount of money, dedicate no more than twenty seconds to noting down:

- The date
- The amount
- The category of spending (eating out, coffee, clothes, entertainment, groceries, etc.)
- Optionally, a description of what you bought

Don't worry about recurring costs like subscriptions or big regular ones like your mortgage, energy bills, travel costs or gym membership: you'll get to those in the next step. The aim here is just to reduce the steady drip of daily spending by making yourself more mindful of it.

You might expect that there's a step coming up where you review what you've spent and when. Nope. If you want to, you can shred your notes at the end of each day and it won't make the slightest bit of difference. This is the magic of the whole process: just knowing you'll have to write it down will reduce your spending without even trying. More often than you'd expect, you'll subconsciously project forward a couple of minutes and realise you won't feel good about writing it down – so you won't spend the money. (Recording everything you eat, without having a calorie limit, works for the same reason.)

If you think this sounds like an annoyance . . . well, you're right – that's largely the point. But it's not a habit you need to keep up endlessly: after spending a week or two being more mindful around your spending, you'll find that the effect on your behaviour lasts long after you've stopped. It won't last for ever, though – so you might want to repeat the exercise next time your credit card bill gives you a scare.

Step 3: Use the 'two-week rule'

Step 2 does a great job of naturally curtailing the day-to-day drip of small purchases, and you can supplement it with a trick to make sure any bigger purchases you make will significantly improve your life.

The two-week rule is simple. When you decide you really must have a new phone, a fancy accessory for your bike, a juicer, or anything that costs more than, say, £30, tell yourself: 'Self, you can totally have this – no worries! You've just got to wait a couple of weeks.'

The Saving Myth

You'll be astonished how often the burning desire completely evaporates before the two-week wait is up. I had this recently with an iPad: I became completely obsessed with how it would revolutionise my reading and note-taking, and got deep into researching specs, features and accessories.

Two weeks later? I wasn't fussed any more. I realised I was fine just reading on my phone – and anyway, could I really be bothered to constantly charge up yet another device?

But what if you do still want this life-changing item at the end of the waiting period? Totally fine! Go ahead, guilt-free. Remember, mindful spending isn't an exercise in self-denial: it's just making sure you don't act on a passing whim and regret it later.

Two weeks works perfectly for me: I can comfortably sustain a burning desire for a week, yet a month seems unreasonably long to wait. You can experiment with this and find the timespan that works best for you.

Step 4: Hold a one-off spending audit

Slash and burn, baby! Now we're getting into the fun zone by wiping a meaningful chunk off your monthly expenses – and, critically, doing so without giving up anything you care about.

This step involves going through your bank statements from the last couple of months and identifying any expenses that can be reduced or eliminated.

Anything that's billed every month – such as subscription services – is perfect for cutting because you'll take a single action now and realise the benefit every month into the future. One-off costs are fair game too, though: you might be stunned by the cost of going to that concert last month (£120 for tickets, £50 for dinner beforehand, £50 for the babysitter) and decide to do fewer outings like that in future.

But remember: only eliminate spending that doesn't make a significant difference to your enjoyment of life. This is about trimming the fat, not denying yourself all earthly pleasures.

If you absolutely loved that concert and you spent weeks anticipating it in the run-up, then it's fine. But we all have habitual spending which – when we sit down to consider it – doesn't move the hedonic needle.

Conservatively, I reckon you'll be able to take 10 per cent off your spending while barely noticing it. You can even set yourself a target to cut by a certain amount, if that makes the exercise a fun challenge for you.

I call this a 'one-off' spending audit, but it's never truly one-and-done: things change and undesirable spending always sneaks back in, so this is an exercise worth conducting once a year. Maybe on your birthday, so it's easy to remember. (Joking. Even I'm not that weird.)

Step 5: Assess your biggest 'fixed' costs

As I mentioned, fixed costs will be responsible for the majority of virtually everyone's spending.

These costs aren't easy to reduce but the impact is huge. For example, say that your housing costs make up 30 per cent of your spending. That means that if you can find a way to reduce your housing costs by a third, you've just reduced your overall expenditure by 10 per cent in one go. That's a lot of lattes. The same logic applies to childcare costs, transport, and any other big fixed costs applicable to your situation.

Approach this step as a brainstorming exercise, where nothing is too crazy to be considered. The best ideas often come from starting at a slightly silly extreme ('I could always sleep under the desk at work') to break out of your current thought pattern, then

The Saving Myth

walking it back to something more moderate ('actually, if I could find a job I could cycle to, it'd save me £200 per month').

By the time you've finished this step, you might have decided to explore:

- Switching to a cheaper mortgage, if one is available.
- Moving closer to work (or moving work closer to home) to eliminate commuting costs.
- Looking for a job where you can work from home more often.
- Starting to commute by bike instead of by car or train.
- Moving to a country or region with a lower cost of living.
- Changing your working patterns so you don't need so many hours of childcare.

There will be lots of other options too, once you put your mind to it. Just don't expect any of them to be easy.

Remember: the point of this exercise is to cut costs without negatively affecting your enjoyment of life. It might be that moving to a cheaper area, for example, would make you miserable – in which case, don't do it. However, most of us end up with our current lifestyle accidentally through a long series of random events and best guesses about what was the right thing to do at the time – so it's well worth taking a fresh look at your fixed costs and generating a list of options to explore.

Step 6: Pay yourself first

Unless you're a wild exception who already had perfectly calibrated spending, after following the first five steps you'll find that you now have more to invest. Now it's time to automate the process of channelling that extra saving into investments – and, critically, making this the first thing that happens as soon as you get paid.

'Pay yourself first' is another concept that's been around for over a hundred years. The idea is simple: you take the amount you want to save, and automatically shift it straight into a dedicated savings account as soon as you get paid. Out of sight, out of mind.

On one level, this is practical: if you treat your savings fund as any other bill and pay it first, you have no choice but to restrict your other spending to what's left over. It prevents you from going on an end-of-month splurge, because the money's already been squirrelled away.

In addition, it's psychological. When you pay yourself last with whatever's left over, you're implicitly making the statement that your savings are the least important use of your money. It's a nice-to-have, if circumstances allow. Paying yourself first flips this: by saving (and later investing) before you even pay for your essential living costs, you're saying that your financial future is your top priority.

The true power move here is to make it a payment you're excited to see leaving your account, because it represents a step towards the future you're aiming for. Most banks allow you to add a description to an automated payment – so you could label it your 'freedom fund', 'life upgrade dividend', or whatever sounds exciting and motivational to you.

Paying yourself first is one of those mind hacks that should stop working if you know you're doing it, but for some reason that never seems to happen. For me, this simple mental re-frame totally changed how I thought about investing: it's automatic, it's unavoidable, and everything else needs to fit around it.

How much should you be 'paying yourself'? The conclusive

answer is 'as much as you can' without becoming a masochist. Yet if you're overly ambitious about how much you put aside, then need to sheepishly raid your savings account with a week still to go until pay day, it will drain your motivation and undermine the whole exercise. So start small – even £10 is better than nothing – then assess each month whether you can increase that amount. At some point, you'll want to be shooting for that much-quoted 10 per cent and, preferably, far beyond. But as we'll see later, even if that's nowhere near achievable today, there are easy steps you can take to get there sooner than you might think.

YOUR THREE FINANCIAL LEVERS

You've thought about it and the yacht is a non-negotiable, your personal chef brings you great joy, and your collection of Old Masters is what gives each day its sparkle.

Or, more realistically, maybe you have fulfilling and enjoyable hobbies that happen to be expensive. Or perhaps you live in a high cost-of-living area where you have great friends and family. That's OK, because while saving is an essential first step, it's by far the weakest lever we can pull to control of our finances.

Why? Well, imagine you're currently earning £50,000, and spending every penny of it. Your goal is to have £10,000 per year left over to put towards investments. Holding your income constant, that would mean cutting your spending by 20 per cent. Possible? Maybe, but not much fun.

The alternative is to make an extra £10,000 by some other means, and hold spending constant. This could be as easy as learning a new skill or applying for a job in a better paying industry – and you'd achieve your goal without any lifestyle sacrifice whatsoever. Not only that, there's nothing to stop you (in theory at least) keeping on going until you achieve an income of £100,000 per year. Now you're saving £50,000 per year, which would clearly have been impossible to achieve without the income boost: however many nights out you skip, coupons you clip and streaming services you cancel, there's a hard limit to how much you can cut back.

This means that if you can find a way to keep nudging your income upwards, you don't need to worry too much about how much you're saving today. For example, say you're earning £50,000 and sticking to the standard advice of saving 10 per cent of what you earn: £5,000. Next year, you secure a pay rise so you're earning £55,000 – meaning that if you stuck to the 10 per cent rule, you'd now be saving £5,500 and would have an extra £4,500 to spend.

What if instead, though, you split the increase 50/50 between spending and saving? You'd still have an extra £2,500 to spend on whatever you like – but you'd also now be saving £7,500 rather than £5,000 per year. Your savings rate has increased from 10 per cent to 13.6 per cent – without having to cut back, and in fact while spending more than you did before. Next time your earnings increase, you can repeat the trick – again lifting your saving rate while still having more money to enjoy today.

At first it sounds like the least helpful money advice ever, but 'make more money' – combined with mindful spending – is pretty much the ultimate silver bullet when it comes to living a better financial life. And that's why the focus of the rest of this book is not on saving money, but on making more of it.

I like to think of people's finances as the result of three financial levers, each being pulled in the right way. First, there's the subject of this chapter, saving – which is a critical first step, but as we've seen, by far the least effective. The second lever is investing, which captures the imagination because it allows your money to grow without your involvement: earning income from dividends or a rental property is like having a second job, without the tedious business of turning up yourself to earn it. It isn't all upside all the time, but eventually it comes good – and from Chapter 3 onwards we'll explore what investing wisely, without taking on an undue amount of risk, truly entails.

But the most powerful lever by far – dramatically more powerful than investing, yet typically overlooked in mainstream personal finance advice – is the one we'll turn to in the next chapter: earning. And, happily, while there's seldom been a worse time to be a saver, there's never been a better time to increase your earnings.

2

MYTH If you work hard enough today, retirement will be your reward.

REALITY It's more realistic, and more satisfying, to find ways to earn indefinitely – just without the hard work.

CHAPTER 2
THE EARLY RETIREMENT MYTH

Luke Pittard was twenty-three when he won £1.3 million on the lottery. Enough for him to immediately quit his job at his local McDonald's in Cardiff, and enough – if invested wisely – for him to never have to work again.

And at first that was his plan – except it didn't turn out that way. Within a few months Luke started to find his new life of luxury a bit dull: 'To be honest, there's only so much relaxing you can do. I'm only young and a bit of hard work never did anyone any harm.'

Eventually, he went back to his old job. 'I enjoy going to work and all my mates work here,' he said. The only change? Instead of walking to and from work, he now gets a taxi.

Luke isn't alone. Mark Brudenell won nearly a million pounds on the lottery and initially spent three years flying around the world on luxury holidays – but then got bored and set up his own double glazing business. He says he puts 'more hours into the business than I ever did working before', and doesn't even touch the remainder of his lottery winnings. Roy Gibney won £7.5 million and said: 'I gave up work for fourteen years, but I got bored. I started a sheet metal business, and I'm fitter and happier than I've been for years.'

All in all, a third of lottery jackpot winners set up their own business, and almost the same amount again go back to life as an employee. And it's not because they've foolishly blown it all: even if they don't need the money, it turns out that work meets a deep-seated need for meaning and social connection.

This claim would be hotly disputed by advocates of a philosophy that revolves around escaping the world of work as quickly as possible. Catchily entitled FIRE – 'Financial Independence, Retire Early' – it would go from being a fringe lifestyle to a mainstream movement in the wake of the 2007–2008 financial crisis. FIREites preach that you should spend a decade or two working insanely hard and saving the majority of what you earn, build up a big pile of investments, then quit work and live off that pile for ever. The idea is basically to speed run the normal career path: by saving at far above the normal rate (it's not unusual for hardcore FIRE followers to save more than 50 per cent of what they earn), you can retire closer to your fortieth birthday than your sixtieth.

The trouble, as many of those who successfully FIREd themselves discovered, wasn't the self-denial or the performance of the financial markets. It was this: the type of person who has both the type of job (a high paying, high status one) and the motivation to put themselves in a position to retire so young isn't also going to be the type of person who enjoys unbroken decades of endless relaxation. As one fifty-one-year-old FIRE 'success story' put it in a blog post: 'Now I'm living the Early Retirement dream. Guess what? I find myself fantasising about returning to work.' A year of dabbling with badminton, joining a local book club and volunteering at the community garden later, and he did just that.

Don't get me wrong: there are elements of the FIRE philosophy that I strongly agree with, not least its focus on getting out of a job you hate and bringing your financial life under your own control as soon as possible. But its fatal flaw is that it ignores the ample academic research indicating that retirement isn't the rose-tinted dream most of us expect it to be – and can even be disastrous for our mental wellbeing.

For example, researchers from Binghamton University in New York looked at data from rural China, which historically lacked the structured pension provision available in urban areas. In 2009, a pension scheme began to be introduced that aimed to eventually cover all rural areas. But its gradual roll-out proved to be the perfect natural experiment: suddenly, retirement became a possibility for some elderly Chinese citizens but not others. Surely, the researchers assumed, the people who retired would be happier and healthier than those who didn't?

Not quite. In their analysis of more than 17,000 people, the researchers found that, ten years after the introduction of pensions, the rate of cognitive decline had greatly accelerated in the areas where people had been receiving the extra support. And it wasn't just their cognitive abilities that suffered; it was their mood too. 'It looks like the negative effect on social engagement [of retirement] far outweighed the positive effect of the program on nutrition and sleep,' one of the researchers concluded. All in all, the evidence indicates that we shouldn't find the stories of lottery winners as surprising as we do. Retirement, *The Economist* recently summarised, often leads to losses 'of income, purpose or, most poignantly, relevance'.

Except none of this has made much of a dent in the popular belief that we should build our lives around the desire to retire. In the UK and US, policies to increase the age at which you can collect retirement benefits from sixty-five to sixty-seven have been met with much grumbling and resistance. In France, more than a million people took to the streets when the government tried to increase the pension age from sixty-two to sixty-four in 2023. And while governments are trying to push retirement age back, our general perception seems to be that mid-sixties is already rather too late: a study of Millennial Americans put the ideal retirement age at sixty-one.

For many people, early – or at least early-ish – retirement is clearly the ultimate goal. But should it be? The trouble is, as we saw in the last chapter, earning is the most powerful of the three financial levers we have – and so wanting to retire early means less time benefiting from this power as we try to compress our earning into as short a time as possible. If there were another way to think about earning – one that emphasised making money without the endless grind – we might realise that there are some altogether more fulfilling (and lucrative) ways to think about our working lives.

RETIREMENT: A VERY MODERN INVENTION

At first it might seem odd that quitting work leaves us bored, socially isolated and even declining mentally. But to somebody a hundred years ago, the idea of ending our working lives without being forced to do so by illness or injury may have felt more peculiar still. The concept of 'retirement' as a distinct stage of life may be firmly embedded, but it's also surprisingly new.

The very first pension paid as standard to everyone who reached a certain age wasn't introduced until 1883, in Germany. In the UK, it took until 1908 for a state pension to be introduced – and, because it was only available upon turning seventy, only one in four people lived long enough to claim it. In the US, there was no federal provision for mass retirement until 1935, with the introduction of the Social Security Act.

Yet, over a short space of time, retirement expanded rapidly. In 1930, 58 per cent of men over sixty-five were still working; by the year 2000 that number had fallen to 17.5 per cent. That's despite the fact that lifespans were growing over that time: a sixty-five-year-old man in 1930 would (statistically) only expect to live an extra twelve years, whereas now he might have another twenty. In the UK, the most common age of death for a woman is now eighty-nine, by which time she might have spent almost thirty years in retirement.

The Early Retirement Myth

Over the course of a century, we've gone from retirement barely existing to it being the norm – and an aspiration – to spend the final third of our lives not working.

On a societal level, this is clearly unsustainable. In 1955, there were 8.6 Americans of working age for every person in retirement. By 2013, this had fallen to 2.8. If you see deductions made from your payslip being allocated to something reassuring sounding like social security or national insurance, don't get the idea that you're putting money aside for your own dotage: everything you pay in is immediately being handed to people who are receiving retirement benefits today. Your own retirement is dependent on governments successfully adding new debt to their ever-growing piles without the system crumbling: that debt can then be used to pay you out, and the eventual bill will be some future generation's problem.

On a personal level too, ever-longer retirements require heroic levels of savings and astonishingly high investment returns: to retire at sixty, you might need to generate enough from forty years of work to sustain you for another thirty. Even for those who've retired recently – and benefited from their investments being boosted by a decades-long trend of falling interest rates – that's a major stretch. But now that trend has come to an end and future returns are likely to be lower than we've become used to, it feels impossible.

To compound the problem, previous generations could have banked on paying off their house in full by the time they turned sixty – perhaps by taking out a twenty-five-year mortgage at the age of thirty-five. Now, with typical mortgage terms running for longer to keep repayments somewhat affordable despite interest rates being higher, that's far from guaranteed to be the case.

Of course, it's a rare person who wants to be working forty-hour weeks until they drop – and 'I'd be bored out of my mind if I wasn't still working at seventy!' sounds virtuous as a vigorous thirty-something, but in reality none of us knows for how long our health will permit us to stay physically and mentally active.

Yet for economic reasons if nothing else, it seems likely that we'll end up looking at the past century – where people came to expect to spend the final decades of their lives devoted wholly to leisure – as an historical anomaly. It was enabled by a rare set of economic and demographic conditions that have now passed, and which we may never see again.

Many of us simply won't be able to punch out of our jobs for the last time on our fortieth (or even sixty-sixth) birthday. But here's the thing: if you can find the right approach to earning, you might come to see a longer working life as a source of excitement rather than despair.

Just as with the over-emphasis on saving that we encountered in the previous chapter, the preoccupation with early retirement is another example of formerly good advice that's become dangerously misguided as the world has changed. When most people's work was mainly physical, having a defined end date made sense. But now that most of us are paid based on our mental and social contributions – and our lifespans are longer – the idea of drifting off into several golden decades without work isn't just socially unsustainable, but personally undesirable.

Because, for most people, the problem with work isn't the entire concept of work: it's full-time work, or work that means you miss your kids' bedtime, or work that involves being nice to people you can't stand, or work that stresses you out because your fate is in someone else's hands. The FIRE movement had it half right: Financial Independence is a great goal – it's just that the second half of their stated aim, Retiring Early, probably isn't.

The solution isn't to escape the world of work as early as you can, or to cross your fingers and pray for a lottery win: it's to find a way to sustainably live a dream life that has income-generation built into it. It's not giving up on earning, but finding ways to earn that don't monopolise your time. And, fortunately, there are ways to keep on making money well into your seventies and beyond – offering all the leisure and free time we now associate with retirement, plus a dollop of extra personal satisfaction and mental reward on top.

BREAKING THE TIME–MONEY CONNECTION

On Reddit, 279,000 people are members of a community called 'Overemployed'. Its contributors have figured out that they're able to meet the basic requirements of their job in half of a conventional working week – so rather than scrolling social media like the rest of us, they've taken on a second job to fill the other half.

Some take it even further. One user racked up four jobs, then quit one – complaining of 'too many meetings'. Another has five 'full-time' jobs in tech, adding up to nearly a million dollars in combined salary. One user summed up the sentiment of the subreddit: 'don't have to be perfect, no need to be the best, just do enough . . . And coast.'

Of course, this is only possible because they're doing it covertly. If their bosses knew how efficiently they were fulfilling their duties, they wouldn't be delighted – they'd be horrified, and probably cut their working days (and pay) in half. That sentiment is understandable: most of us instinctively feel that sneakily holding down two jobs at once is wrong. When you think about it, though, if they can provide enough full-time value to satisfy two (or more) companies at once, why shouldn't they? It's not their fault they're not working at capacity: if their boss is happy, why should they ask for more work or twiddle their thumbs?

The reason working two jobs simultaneously feels so immoral is our deeply ingrained sense that time is money. We're used to compensation being based either explicitly on an hourly rate, or on being paid a salary with the assumption that you'll be working a particular number of hours.

Yet why should pay be determined by the hours you work rather than the value you provide? If your car has broken down and it takes the repair guy five minutes to fix it, you don't calculate a 'reasonable' hourly rate and try to pay a twelfth of it: you're grateful he got you back on the road so quickly and pay whatever he demands. It took Ed Sheeran less than half an hour to write 'Thinking Out Loud', and he's earned millions from that song alone. Does that feel unreasonable to you? Would you tap your toe more vigorously if he'd slaved over it for weeks?

These examples hint at another way to think about work, earnings and retirement. There is a way to keep earning money easily, without having to set an arbitrary retirement goal – and it involves breaking the connection between time and money altogether.

The key to breaking the connection is what I call 'the impact equation'. This equation states that the amount of money you earn is made up of the value you provide, multiplied by the number of people you provide it to. Having your car fixed is valuable to you, and having it fixed quickly is more valuable than having it fixed slowly. The impact of a pop song is low to any single person, but becomes significant when multiplied out across millions of people across time. You make more money when you offer more value to the same number of people, or the same amount of value to a large number of people – or, ideally, both.

Admittedly, you don't need to search too hard for cases where the equation seems to break down. Nurses and teachers come to mind: they serve a lot of people and it's hard to think of any other work that makes such a directly positive impact on people's lives, yet they're typically not on the waiting list for the new

The Early Retirement Myth

Ferrari. But this is because, within the constraints of employment, the impact equation doesn't apply: distortions, unfairness, convention and a hundred other factors can result in value being underpriced, unrecognised or it benefiting someone other than the person who created it.

But, by sidestepping traditional employment, it becomes possible to manipulate the impact equation to earn vastly more – even in the most chronically undervalued professions. Rachel Accurso, for example, does pretty much what any other preschool teacher does – but she does it on YouTube as 'Ms Rachel', where she has 7 million subscribers and is estimated to earn up to $15 million per year. Digital distribution allowed her to provide value to more people, shifting the equation in her favour. Or take Mike Linares, who at one point was a nurse at a Los Angeles hospital who'd failed his professional exams countless times. Once he hit upon a successful study method, he started coaching peers on the side – and because passing quickly is extremely valuable to people who need the qualification to unlock a better job, it eventually became a series of study guides that now generates more than a million dollars per year.

Rachel and Mike have both broken the time–money connection by hacking the impact equation. They don't need to work hard if they don't want to: they're earning extremely well, and could cut back considerably while still earning dramatically more than the average person. They don't need to forgo holidays: whether they work this week or not, they still get paid. And they certainly don't need to retire early: they love what they do, so they can do it for ever.

Admittedly, they are outliers: not everyone will achieve their level of success. But nor do they need to. After all, if you could just earn as much as you do now while enjoying what you do and without needing to work anything close to forty hours a week, would you still feel under pressure to retire by a certain date?

THE THREE LEVELS OF FINANCIAL INDEPENDENCE

OK, this all sounds great – but how do you do it? Well, I think of financial independence not as a result, but a process: one that typically involves moving through three levels.

Level 1: Embrace the connection

Inevitably, for most of us time and money start off being inextricably linked. You might only be paid once you've punched in and the clock starts ticking, or be required to sit in an office between certain hours if you want to keep your job (and therefore your salary). If you can work from home and sneak in the odd laundry load on company time, you're one of the lucky ones.

But employment isn't all bad. Think of it as an apprenticeship: a period during which you'll have certainty about when and how much you'll be paid, and be able to build your skills and hone your craft by getting involved in big projects with talented people. It's a step that – even if we dream of escaping it from depressingly early on – most of us benefit from. Even if you graduated top of your class from a prestigious university, when you move on to any real-world job you'll start out being pretty crap at it. If you lived or died by your results, you'd probably die – so having some leeway to learn while still getting paid is exactly what you need. Even beyond the early stages of your career, there's a benefit in learning from the people around you and getting in plenty of 'reps' at whatever you've chosen as the skill or area you want to master.

Yes, I'm painting the rosiest possible picture of the world of work here. Most people don't float through the office door on a cloud of gratitude for all the opportunities they're exposed to: they feel under-appreciated, sick of playing politics, and resentful.

The Early Retirement Myth

But there are ways to maximise your opportunities in Level 1 while preparing yourself to move to Level 2: to be precise, three of them.

1: Re-frame

Most people, explicitly or implicitly, see their career as something that happens 'to' them, based on the actions of other people. Your boss won't give you a raise. You're stuck on a dead-end project. Your ideas are always overlooked. If a better opportunity comes along, it's pure luck.

The first step is to re-frame your career as something you're in control of, and approach it strategically. You're giving up a large proportion of your waking hours: what are you getting in return? If the answer is 'not enough', then you need to honestly assess whether you're worth enough or whether you're currently in the wrong place. Remember, your time in employment is your apprenticeship – and it falls upon you to get the most out of it. What would you be doing differently if you were taking absolute responsibility for acquiring the skills you need to escape?

In the academic literature this sense of personal responsibility is known as 'career self-efficacy', and research from around the world has demonstrated its powerful effects. In one study, academics in Germany followed more than 700 people from the point of graduation, and found that high self-efficacy translated into better pay and higher work satisfaction seven years later. This is not the same as deluding yourself that everything about your job is within your control: in reality, other people do have an influence and some things will affect you unfairly. You will, sometimes, be overlooked for a promotion because someone else has bonded with the boss over drinks after work, for example.

You don't need to stare at yourself in the mirror and repeat 'I am the prize!' every morning, but merely acting as if everything is within your control will improve your results.

2: Keep learning

Your ability to break the time–money connection will rest upon the value of the skills you have developed. Some of these will come naturally from experience – but there are a few specific areas you can focus on to speed you towards Level 2, and give your earnings an immediate boost too.

One of these is to learn specialist skills that can lead you into particularly well-paying areas of your field. For example, according to a global report on the link between skills and earnings, IT professionals who earn a new certification can increase their salary by $12,000 or more. That's one heck of a premium for taking a training course or doing some self-study. Similarly, a report from The Project Management Institute (who, I admit, may not be a wholly disinterested party) found that those with a project management qualification earn 22 per cent more than those who lack one. Whichever line of work you're in, there will likely be an equivalent.

You can also develop 'soft skills' that transfer across roles and industries – and will also stand you in good stead if you strike out on your own when we move on to Level 2. For example, a study from the University of California found that people who demonstrated leadership skills early in life earned up to 33 per cent more as adults, even after controlling for differences in intelligence and other traits. Separately, a study of more than 42,000 people by TalentSmart found that employees with high emotional intelligence (EQ) earned an average of $29,000 more per year than those with low EQ.

How do you develop these skills? While there are formal courses and qualifications out there, the most effective way of learning is a mix of deliberate self-study (like reading books or listening to podcasts) and seizing opportunities to learn on the job. This is why re-framing is a critical first step: by mentally taking ownership of your career, you'll spot development opportunities that otherwise would have passed you by.

With minimal extra learning, you might even be able to take a strategic side-step. For example, data from the US Bureau of Labor Statistics shows that journalists earn a median wage of $49,300, whereas for public relations specialists it's $66,750. The skills involved? Very similar – I used to work in public relations, and journalists would move across to join us on 'the dark side' all the time, relying on their existing knowledge and networks.

3: Forget loyalty

An analysis of 18 million employment records by Yahoo Money found that job switchers routinely increased their pay by significantly more than those who stayed put. The reason doesn't take much figuring out. When a company is hiring a new employee, they have no choice but to pay the market rate for someone with their desired level of skills and experience. Yet when they want to retain an existing employee, they can rely on inertia. If someone enjoys their job and earns some kind of pay rise, are they really going to bother looking around? Do they even know they'd earn more if they were newly hired into their current role?

Of course, happiness is important: if you like where you work, you might not want to take the risk of leaving for a role you end up hating. But you don't need to leave; you just need to keep looking around. For a start, actively looking will give you a sense of what you could or should be earning in your current role: if your company was hiring a replacement for you, how much would they pay? If you're not being rewarded with the pay rises you think you should be, you can then take it a step further: be offered a role elsewhere, then ask your employer to match it if they want you to stay.

Put starkly, the key to higher earnings is to put yourself in a position where your employer needs you more than you need them. In every company there are a few people who by handing in their resignation could cause the CEO to cancel their plans for the day and throw everything at getting them to change their mind. Your aim is to be this person.

This largely comes down to solving problems that other people can't (or won't), and being a 'safe pair of hands'. The person in my company who's risen through the ranks the fastest got there because she got the job done every single time – without drama or complaint. Every time a new area of responsibility came along it ended up with her, because we knew for sure it'd be done well. Sometimes that meant her working late, or scrambling to figure something out that she'd never done before – but it was worth it, because she made herself irreplaceable.

Making these three changes will shift the impact equation in your favour: you'll be adding more value, and capturing more of it for yourself. The difference this makes to your earning power in the next three to five years could be enormous. As we've seen, earning is by far the most powerful lever you have – so taking a deliberate approach to your career can have a bigger impact than decades of disciplined saving or any amount of effort to transform yourself into an investing genius.

It might be that taking these steps is enough for you: you'll be earning more, and be in a position to call the shots. This transformed power dynamic and a newly padded payslip may keep you happily clocking in all the way to the typical retirement age and beyond. But if you do want to go further, the skills you've developed have set you up perfectly for Level 2.

The Early Retirement Myth

Level 2: Loosen the connection

When Steve Jobs left Apple to start his new company, NeXT, he needed a logo. Being Steve Jobs, he wanted the best – so he approached legendary designer Paul Rand.

Rand knew his value: he demanded a fee of $100,000. There would be no consultation, and no revisions: he'd receive $100,000, deliver what he thought was the best visual concept, and that would be it. Jobs agreed – and Rand received $100,000 for two weeks' work. (If you ask me, the logo was pretty awful, but that's by the by.)

This is an extreme example of loosening the connection between time and money. Rand did, at some point, have to sit down and do the work. He did need to deliver by a particular deadline. But he didn't send Steve Jobs an invoice listing the number of hours he'd worked: he was selling the result rather than selling his time.

A less extreme example of someone operating at Level 2 is my friend Richard. After twenty years working in finance roles at major banks, he struck out on his own as a consultant. He still sells his time – but as a consultant he sells it by the day, not as part of a salary. And because he's proven himself to be able to deliver a certain result during that time, his day rate is what he likes to call 'reassuringly expensive'.

At the moment, he consults for a couple of different companies for a total of three days per week. Every weekend is a long one, which – along with breaks between contracts – allows him to routinely rack up the type of unforgettable experiences that would normally have to wait until 'retirement'. If his travel plans require more cash, he can take on more work for a bit – yet when he wanted to take the whole summer off and live on a Greek island, he did. As anyone at Level 1 can attest, it's rare to be able to achieve this level of flexibility from the outset of your career:

when what you're primarily selling is a result, you need to have demonstrated beyond doubt your ability to deliver that result on someone else's terms before you get to do it on your own.

Operating independently doesn't just bring more flexibility – consultants tend to be paid at least 20 per cent more than an employee in an equivalent position, and sometimes more than 50 per cent. Some of this difference disappears due to taxes and costs that would otherwise fall on the employer, but even so – operating at Level 2 gives you the potential to earn a lot more. The trade-off is a lack of certainty, which is a big reason why the pay differential exists in the first place. After all, you need to charge enough to compensate for vacations and time off sick (which you won't be paid for), and to cover times when you can't find work.

If you want to make the move to Level 2, you'll need to plan ahead to make sure you have experience in the type of role that's suited to being done as a contractor. Not all roles are. In the corporate world there are a lot of jobs that exist in the context of a particular company because of the way it operates, but not anywhere else – so you could be phenomenal at it, but struggle to find other clients. There are also sectors, like investment banking or sensitive government roles, where you'll have access to the kind of proprietary information that means an employer wouldn't be happy to have you working elsewhere simultaneously or soon afterwards.

All this means that the roles most suited to Level 2 are those where you're selling a distinct result or providing a widely understood and in-demand service. Project-based work is perfect, because the defined end point means it often won't make sense to hire someone in-house. This is common in design, IT and marketing, as well as other fields. And although it might not seem like it, the more specific your area of expertise, the better – because you'll be one of very few people who can be hired to solve a specific problem. For example, my friend Mark is one of about five people in the country who understand an ancient programming language that major banks (worryingly) still rely on. This means he can pretty much name his price – whereas if he looked for work as a generalist IT contractor, he'd be competing in a deeper labour market with clearer norms around pay.

Once you're in a role that lends itself to consulting, the easiest way of getting started – and an extremely common one – is to get hired as a consultant by the company you already work for. But beyond that first role, you'll need to put yourself out there. This takes you into the unavoidable and often uncomfortable world of 'business development': speaking to other people in the industry, showcasing your expertise, and letting it be known that you're available. For most roles there are agencies and recruiters who can help find you work, but this isn't something you want to rely on. As time goes on, finding new roles becomes easier because you build a larger pool of colleagues you've worked alongside who can mention your name when something comes up: among the many consultants I know, word-of-mouth is by far the most common way to find work. This may sound extreme, but you might even need to start using LinkedIn . . .

I hope I haven't made this transition sound straightforward, because it's anything but: it's scary to voluntarily give up a secure income stream and not know when you'll get paid again. But once you've established yourself, Level 2 is a pretty great place to be. There's nothing to stop you from hanging out at this level for ever, with no need to think about retirement as a one-off 'event' because you're free to scale your volume of work up and down to match your energy levels and fit in with whatever else you want to do. But if you're up for taking another leap, you can graduate to Level 3: breaking the link between time and money altogether.

Level 3: Break the connection

The core requirement to reach Level 3 is to be able to deliver a result in a form that's completely independent of your own time.

For example, if you're a physical therapist specialising in shoulder pain, there's only so much you can get paid for a session of digging your thumbs into someone's trapezius – and only so many sessions you can do per day before you develop serious RSI.

But what if you could take your knowledge and package it up into a book that allowed someone to get the same relief at home by using some simple tools and following the steps you'd take? By doing so, you've largely broken the link between time and money: you may still need to promote it or be involved in its distribution, but you could take weeks or months off without your income being affected.

You could even formalise your unique 'method' and teach it to other therapists – requiring them to pay training and licensing fees. Eventually you could end up with multiple divisions and product lines, and hire dedicated teams to help with marketing, distribution, operations and finance. There's a limit – albeit a high one – to how much even the most sought-after professional (such as Paul Rand and his logo design) can earn in a year, and only so many years they can consistently deliver for. But once you're selling a product that doesn't require your personal input, there are no such constraints. You build it once, then sell it countless times.

There are ways to break the time–money connection in almost every sector. For example, Rachel Karten worked in social media at some of the most popular food and recipe websites. Then she made her move to Level 2 – transitioning to independent social media consulting, helping other companies to achieve the same results that she'd previously generated in-house and passing on her knowledge so they could continue doing it even after she'd moved on. Finally, she started *Link in Bio* – a paid newsletter and private community that teaches those same techniques at scale without Rachel needing to show up and do it one-on-one by the hour. That's Level 3. She's now estimated to be making more than $200,000 per year, and if she wants to earn more it won't necessarily require any more of her time.

Or take Ben Collins, a former forensic accountant. I don't know much about accounting, but I know it involves a lot of spreadsheets – and after quitting his job he started picking up consulting work showing companies how to build performance-tracking dashboards in Google Sheets. Two years later, he packaged up this knowledge into a course that people can buy online, meaning Ben gets paid at all hours of the day and night, even when he's out hiking with his family. Even if Ben never creates another course or takes on another consulting gig, he'll keep on getting paid.

In each case the skill involved and delivery mechanism is different but the core principle is the same: identifying a result you know how to achieve and other people want, then packaging it up in a way that doesn't involve your time every time.

That doesn't mean once you've created something you'll never work again: especially in the early days, most people find themselves working harder than ever to grow and stabilise a business of this kind. But there are two important differences compared to working equally hard at Level 1 and Level 2. The first is that the financial return on your time can be dramatically higher: if you slave away late into the night on a marketing initiative that improves sales by 10 per cent, you'll continue to reap the rewards of that 10 per cent increase for years to come. Potentially, you can end up earning thousands of pounds for one hour of work. The second important difference is you can do all this entirely on your schedule: not only can Ben and Rachel work on any days and times that suit them, they can also take extended blocks of time off without forgoing any income or asking anyone's permission.

Say that you build a tiny one-person business that brings in £1,000 per month (£12,000 per year). That probably doesn't sound life-changing. But if you assume that a financial investment in real estate or the stock market would pay you an annual return of 5 per cent, your £1,000 in monthly income is equivalent to having £240,000 saved up and invested.

Is it going to be quicker and easier to package up a result and generate £1,000 per month or to build up nearly a quarter of a million pounds in savings? Personally, I think it's the former – and it also gives you a far higher level of control. With that money coming in independently of your time, who cares if the markets don't perform so well or your house doesn't go up in value as much as you'd hoped?

Work less, earn more

For the purposes of getting the concept across, I've made the process of breaking the link between time and money sound like a simple, predictable progression. In reality, it's no such thing. Whatever you try first probably won't succeed. If you plug away for years at something – or skip between multiple ideas – without gaining any traction, that's entirely normal.

But this isn't a case of either/or: once you have the ability to provide a result that people want, you can work on your Level 3 solution simultaneously with Levels 1 and 2. Because it will inevitably take time to figure out, the earlier you start the better – even if that just means spending a few hours per week learning new skills, researching the market and taking your first steps. And even if the worst happens, and you never succeed at all? You still haven't really lost: the skills you'll learn from trying will make you more valuable in your career and so you'll position yourself for a boost in pay compared to your less enterprising colleagues anyway. By progressively weakening the connection between time and money – and perhaps eventually breaking it completely – all concerns about retirement become irrelevant. There's no need to scrimp and save to extreme levels. No worries about your investments failing to perform. And no need to step off the career ladder only to suffer the mental downsides of a retirement that wasn't, in fact, quite as rewarding as you'd expected.

3

MYTH The correct way to invest involves reducing risk as much as possible.

REALITY There is no 'correct' way to invest – it's up to you to find an approach that matches your motivations (including the one that traditional models ignore).

CHAPTER 3
THE RISK-MINIMISATION MYTH

In 2005, Ashvin Chhabra was wrestling with a question: given that the 'optimal' way of structuring an investment portfolio had been known for over fifty years, why did no one actually use it?

Chhabra was an executive at the investment bank Merrill Lynch, and would go on to manage the money of one of the world's most successful investors and biggest philanthropists. Many of the bank's clients had, by any reasonable measure, already won the game of money – and given that they were taking professional advice, you might expect their investments to be a case study in sober, sensible risk reduction.

Not a bit of it. No matter how financially sophisticated, these wealthy clients were just as emotional about money as anyone else. When the market was crashing, they rushed for safety and wanted to sell. When the market was booming, they got greedy. And even though they could pretty much stick their money in a savings account and live off the interest, they continued to take risks.

This isn't a dysfunction of the wealthy few with an insatiable lust for more: there's no shortage of people who politely nod along as a financial advisor recommends investing in a carefully crafted selection of stocks and bonds, only to rush out to find a house to flip for a quick profit.

This is because while there is a mathematically 'correct' way to invest, it doesn't fully represent what people really want. Yet, as Chhabra eventually found, there is a completely different approach to investment – one that doesn't imply there's a right answer to be found, but rather appreciates that every investor is looking for something different.

THE THREE MONEY MOTIVATIONS

The textbook way to invest that Chhabra had learned was developed by Harry Markowitz in 1952. Markowitz, essentially, used all manner of fancy maths to work out how an investor should maximise their return without taking on an unacceptable amount of risk. 'Risk', in this model, is the same as 'volatility' – meaning swings in performance from year to year. According to the model, shooting for higher returns involves opening yourself up to more volatility (or risk), so each investor should focus on finding the 'sweet spot' where the return they achieve is as high as possible, but stop short of the point where the sleepless nights would kick in. The working assumption was that every investor wanted the smoothest possible ride and would only take on additional risk if they absolutely needed to.

At the time, modelling this trade-off mathematically was a major breakthrough, and would eventually earn Markowitz the Nobel Prize for Economics in 1990. Since its publication, it's become firmly established as the bedrock of how professional investment portfolios are built.

Yet while it was a valuable contribution to the attempt to solve the investment puzzle, it doesn't come close to addressing how people think about money in the real world. Sure, most of us would prefer an investment that grows in value by a steady, predictable amount rather than one that lurches sickeningly around all over the place – but volatility isn't the only risk. What about the risk of your assets being tied up so you can't access them when you want to? Or that some unforeseen catastrophe means your returns deviate dramatically from those predicted by

The Risk-Minimisation Myth

the model, leaving you high and dry? In the Markowitz model these 'downside risks' don't get a look in.

Chhabra noticed something else crucial: as well as the risk of losing, there's such a thing as the risk of 'failing to win'. In other words, even though his bank's clients were already life's winners (having so much wealth you need someone to help you manage it is the definition of 'nice problem to have'), they weren't preoccupied with avoiding loss. Rationally – and the Markowitz model makes the assumption that investors are rational – they needed merely to avoid doing something very stupid and they'd be able to live a comfortable life for ever. And yet they still wanted to *win*.

This 'winning' motivation – the drive to improve their financial standing, even from a starting position comfortably within the top 1 per cent – was what Chhabra identified as being missing from most financial planning. And if the already-wealthy wanted to win, surely that would also be the case for those further down the wealth distribution ladder, where the results would be more directly life-changing.

In fact, Chhabra identified that there were three separate and competing motivations present in every investor's mind:

- **Protect** against disaster ('personal risk')
- **Maintain** your lifestyle ('market risk')
- **Improve** your financial status ('aspirational risk')

These three motivations aren't listed in order of importance: everyone has them in different proportions, and they even vary in importance for the same individual over time. The key point is that everyone has, to some degree, all the motivations all the time.

Markowitz focused on the second of these: you could use his

model to maintain your lifestyle by solving market risk in the neatest way possible, and if you wanted protection you could get that from cash. Where Chhabra was unique was recognising that, for many people – regardless of wealth level – the third risk of not achieving their aspirational goals was very real, and needed to be balanced alongside the other two.

This explains why billionaires continue to make risky investments when they could live perfectly well without ever earning another penny: they want to keep on winning, and gain ground among their rarefied peer group. After all, how can life be bearable on a 60ft yacht if all your friends suddenly have 80ft yachts with a helipad?

Chhabra's write-up of his research has been cited in later academic papers fewer than a thousand times, compared to Markowitz's 66,000 (and Nobel medal). But I've made it the cornerstone of how I think about investing – and I believe it's more important today than ever before.

During the era of guaranteed final-salary pensions and affordable houses, 'average' was pretty good. Of course, everyone would still like to do better if they could, but if being slap-bang in the middle of the income distribution guaranteed you a paid-off house, a couple of holidays per year and a comfortable retirement? Well, for the more risk-averse members of society that would dampen down the desire to take any chances with the aim of making a big leap upwards.

But in recent years the quality of 'average' has deteriorated: the typical person is less likely to be able to own a home near the start of their working life, less likely to have an adequately funded pension at the end, and their household is more likely to require two incomes to get by.

Then there's investment returns. From 1972 until 2019, an investor in a 60/40 mix of global stocks and bonds would have enjoyed an average annual return of 7.5 per cent, with a standard deviation – a classic measure of volatility – of 10.3 per cent. The most rewarding part of this period coincided with the age of free money: between 2008 and 2020, when most global interest rates were close to zero, investment returns reached as high as 9.6 per cent with barely any rise in volatility.

But this era is gone. From 2020 until mid-2024, the average return from the same portfolio fell to 5.1 per cent while volatility increased to 14 per cent. In this new economic environment – with likely lower investment returns, and less ability to invest at all because the cost of everyday life leaves little left over – more people may feel the motivation to turn up the 'improve' dial. They have less to worry about losing, and staying where they are feels a lot less appealing. This explains why so many young people have been YOLO-ing into meme stocks, and it might not be as irrational as it seems: they might be looking at the vast gap between their grim prospects and what they aspire to, and deciding it's more scary to accept being stuck where they are than to risk losing some money and be set further back.

These are the sorts of tough choices ever more people will need to make. It will be a rare person who can invest enough to simultaneously assure their safety, make incremental gains, and still have some left over to risk on securing a big win. In our new era, the three motivations have never been harder to balance – and it's never been more important to understand them.

UNDERSTANDING THE THREE MOTIVATIONS

Let's dig a bit deeper into each of the three motivations. You'll certainly relate to one more than the others, but you should recognise all of them within yourself to at least some extent.

Motivation #1: Protect against disaster

You don't want to end up having to drastically cut back if you lose your job, if you get ill, or if the economy takes an unprecedented dive. In short, you don't want your financial life to be fragile: you want to put a bit of bubble wrap around it, so you can take some knocks throughout the journey.

For one person, a setback might mean the risk of ending up on a friend's sofa. For another, it might mean yanking the kids out of private school. One is objectively worse than the other, but both will feel painful to the individuals involved: any reduction in lifestyle hurts, even if you're starting from a privileged position.

You therefore want a plan that gives you the near certainty of safety: any upside would be lovely, but not if it risks you taking a big fall from where you are now.

Motivation #2: Maintain your lifestyle

Wouldn't it be great to ditch work completely without having to cut back at all? This is the motivation to maintain your lifestyle, even as you ease off on work – using investment income to replace the income you earn.

Even if we're at peace with the idea of earning money for longer without necessarily retiring, most of us would still like at least the option of stopping work completely and continuing to enjoy the same home, holidays and leisure we do now. And, of course, although it may not be pleasant to think about, there will come a point when we're unable to work at all. So, just as we want near certainty of being protected, we also want a high probability of being able to maintain our lifestyle late in life: any plan that offers just a 50/50 chance would be entirely unacceptable.

Traditional investment portfolios, paired with the protection of owning a house, are designed to get you to that point slowly, predictably and unexcitingly by compounding gradually over time. The smaller the swings in your net worth from year to year along the way, the more successful a financial professional would consider the plan to be.

These two motivations are worthy aims, and I can't imagine anyone who wouldn't want to achieve both. But as Chhabra found, most of us also aspire to something more.

Motivation #3: Improve your financial status

Nobody plays the lottery because they dream of being able to think 'Wow, I guess I'm really safe now!' They also want to move to a bigger house in a nicer area, take more holidays and buy fancier stuff. Some feel the desire to improve their lifestyle more than others, but it's a rare person who's 100 per cent content with what they have and wouldn't be even the tiniest bit interested in giving their life an upgrade.

If we're being honest with ourselves, we also want to improve our position relative to our peers. The American journalist H. L. Mencken once quipped that a wealthy man is one who earns $100 a year more than his wife's sister's husband – and academic research suggests that he was more correct than he might have realised. 'Social comparison theory', pioneered by Leon Festinger in the 1950s, describes the fact that poor people can be happier than wealthy people if they're relatively well-off by the standards of their surroundings. In 2021, Michael Kraus and Jacinth Tan replicated this finding by analysing studies with a total of 2.3 million participants. They showed conclusively that doing objectively well isn't enough, and nor is improving over time or having a better life than your parents: to be happy, you need to be doing at least as well as your peers. In other words, we're all motivated to make a leap up the income distribution scale.

Unfortunately, this pretty much dooms us to perpetual dissatisfaction, because if you suspect that you're surrounded by people who are richer, happier and better looking than you are . . . you're probably right. In fact, this is a phenomenon that has been scientifically proven too, in this case by network scientists Young-Ho Eom and Hang-Hyun Jo. In 2014, the pair introduced what they call the 'generalised friendship paradox'. The paradox is this: most of us have a small number of friends, but a small number of people have a much larger number. It tends to be the case that the people with a larger number of friends also tend to be the ones who are wealthier and happier. As a consequence, each of us is dramatically more likely to find ourselves hanging out with the wealthier, happier people than with more representative types – because it's the rich, happy people who tend to have the biggest networks. Cue endless negative comparisons with our millionaire friends.

All this means that the drive to be more successful than your peers is every bit as deep-rooted as the desire to protect yourself from disaster. But if you confess your hankering to fly first class or start shopping at Harrods to a financial advisor, they're likely to politely redirect you towards a projection of retirement annuity rates and start talking about life insurance.

This is partly because striving to improve your lifestyle involves taking on some degree of risk – and as we've seen, their models tell them that risk is solely there to be minimised. It's also because it's exceptionally difficult to give advice about making big financial leaps. Why so tough? Well, there are a thousand different ways of achieving it, depending on your individual skills and preferences. You can't just tweak a few variables and point to a plan that will suit almost everyone, accompanied by reassuring historical data to show how well it would have done in the past. There's also no guarantee it will work at all: while we demand a high probability of success from the other motivations, significantly improving our financial standing is never going to be more than an alluring possibility. What's more, there's a risk that if we push too hard, we could jeopardise the other two critical motivations.

So it's understandable that this motivation ends up being ignored, but it's a problem – because the important psychological need for striving, improvement and winning isn't being met. It explains why it isn't hard to imagine someone nodding sagely along to the most softly-softly advice in *The Richest Man In Babylon* before flicking across to their investment app and buying the latest hot stock they saw mentioned in their group chat. Anyone with the ambition to improve their status in life – which includes, at the last count, pretty much everyone – is left to figure it out on their own.

THE ONLY INVESTMENT DECISION YOU NEED TO MAKE

Thankfully, by acknowledging and understanding these three competing motivations, we hold the key to radically simplifying our investment decisions. That's because any investment you make will serve one – and only one – of the three motivations.

For example, a cash emergency fund serves the motivation to 'protect'. A speculative investment in a new cryptocurrency is very much powering the drive to 'improve'. It gets more granular too: a diversified mix of stock market investments ticks the 'maintain' box, whereas holding shares in a single company in the hopes it'll shoot up in value is 'improve' all the way.

Once you start seeing the world in this way it makes your investing life almost ridiculously simple, because it reduces the whole complicated business to just one decision: how do I want to balance each of the three motivations?

That's because finding the right balance between these

'buckets' is vastly more important than what you have within each bucket. For example: should you buy your home, or invest in short-term government bonds, or just keep your cash in the bank? Well, as we'll see, they're all 'protect' assets – so if that's the bucket you want to fill, which you pick doesn't matter all that much. Any of them will suit you better than buying an investment property with a mortgage, which falls under 'improve'. It's a bit like choosing between a holiday in Spain, Saint Lucia or the Seychelles: you might prefer one to the others, but they'll all be far better than Siberia if you're in the mood for a beach holiday.

Let's not get carried away, though: just because we've reduced investing to a single decision doesn't mean it's going to be an easy one. How should you be sizing each of those buckets? I have some practical pointers to share – but, first, it's worth looking at some of the factors we need to consider.

The first is where you're starting from. The wealthier you are, the more risks you can afford to take. A billionaire could comfortably have 80 per cent of their assets in the risky 'Improve' bucket. Why? Because 20 per cent of a billion (200 million) invested in the safer buckets would easily be enough to keep them (and their yachts) afloat if everything else went wrong. That doesn't mean all billionaires should take this kind of risk – becoming relatively worse off is painful even if you're still richer than 99.99 per cent of other people. The point is that the more you're starting with, the more risks you can take if you want to.

Then there's your age – or more accurately, your earning potential. Most financial advice is tailored by age, and to an extent this makes sense. Having 20 per cent of your portfolio's value wiped out by some misfortune when you're twenty-five years old is no fun – but at sixty-five years old, when you're on the cusp of retirement, it could be disastrous. As a result, the typical investing advice you'll receive is to gradually shift the balance of your portfolio away from risk as you get older. The trouble is that this approach is a tad simplistic. It's not age that matters, really, but future earnings.

Clearly, as a shortcut, a twenty-year-old is likely to generate more future earnings than a sixty-year-old. In reality, though, two people in their twenties can be on entirely different financial trajectories. Based on age alone, you'd give them both the same financial plan – probably involving building up some savings ('Protect') before making cautious, low-risk investments ('Maintain'). But as it turns out, one of these people is a newly qualified doctor. She has millions of pounds of future earning potential, so she can afford to take some aggressive risks with her money. Even if she loses it all, she potentially has decades of high earnings ahead to make sure she recovers. The other person has no qualifications, and is working in a minimum-wage job. It's still possible for him to end up wealthy (perhaps by starting a business), but he just can't afford to take the same financial risks right now.

Of course, our future doctor might not want to take that kind of risk. That's where the next factor comes in: your fear of loss versus desire for gain.

For example, let's toss a coin. If it comes up 'heads', I'll double whatever cash you have in your bank account right now. But if it lands on 'tails', I'll take half of your bank balance away. This is a good deal in that you stand to gain twice as much as you'd lose. But would you take the bet?

The evidence indicates that most people wouldn't – because we're hard-wired to be more scared of losing money than we're excited by gaining it. This phenomenon – 'loss aversion' – was famously demonstrated by the behavioural economists Amos Tversky and Daniel Kahneman in the 1990s, and is often used to demonstrate that humans are irrational and subject to biases when it comes to investing. However, it only holds for people on average: different people's psychology around money varies wildly.

You can be a risk-taking billionaire or a fearful one. A risk-taking penniless student or a fearful one. There's no right or wrong attitude: it's just a result of how you're wired and the life experiences you've had. But it's worth knowing, because it'll cause you no end of stress if you adopt an approach to investing that's not aligned with your risk tolerance.

HOW TO MAKE THE ONE DECISION

Over the next few chapters, we'll be taking a deeper dive into the assets that fall within each of the three buckets. After that, you'll feel better equipped to decide how much to allocate between them – and when we get there, we'll revisit this question. But it's worth starting with a rough idea now, and I personally think of it in terms of different 'shapes' – each suiting a different type of person and life goal.

> **The pyramid.** The largest share of your investments is in the Protect bucket, followed by Maintain, with a small slice of Improve at the top of the pyramid. This is a common shape that tends to suit people who are happy enough with where they are. They want to stay there without taking much risk, yet without completely giving up on the possibility of a significant change for the better.
>
> **The barbell.** You have the safety of your own home giving you a chunky Protect bucket and, knowing that at least you'll always have a roof over your head, you choose to scrimp on Maintain. Instead, you put the remainder of your cash into Improve assets that attempt to move the needle.
>
> **The fat middle.** You don't own a home (making for a small Protect bucket), and the majority of your investments are of the Maintain variety – with a small amount of Improve on top.

The Risk-Minimisation Myth

The 'T'. Minimal Protect, no Maintain, and almost everything in Improve. This is as risky as it gets, and suits either someone without much to lose or with a burning desire to strike it rich.

You'll probably find yourself drawn to one of these more than the others. But if you don't have a clue which suits you best, it can help to go through the buckets one by one.

Let's start with Improve. A good question to ask yourself is: how much of a risk of loss am I willing to accept in exchange for a shot at a significant gain? Another way of phrasing this, which forces you to face the worst case head-on, is: 'how much would I be willing and able to lose completely?'

At the other end of the spectrum, the size of your Protect bucket will be largely determined by whether you own a home – and whether you want to in the future. Unless you're already wealthy (or, more optimistically, 'until' you're wealthy), the value of your home minus the value of your mortgage will represent a large proportion of your assets. If you're saving up for a home, any cash that forms part of those savings will also form part of your Protect bucket – along with your emergency fund and general savings.

As we'll see in the next chapter, home ownership isn't necessarily right for everyone. If you don't want to own a home in the near future, your Protect bucket will inevitably be smaller – but as you'll have less certainty over your living situation, you might want to balance this out with a larger emergency fund. With these two buckets determined, everything that's left over can be allocated to Maintain.

Important though this decision is, you don't want to overthink it. There's no point removing the 'what should I invest in?' stress only to replace it with 'what size should my buckets be?' stress. It will always be a rough guide rather than an exact target, and it will be continually changing: this may be the only investment decision you need to make but it's one you'll need to revisit on a regular basis.

KEEPING IT SIMPLE

The power of the three motivations lies in the way they simplify investing. Even if you can't decide on quite how to balance your three motivations right now, having it as a framework allows you to sidestep a lot of complexity, guilt-free.

And the financial world does love to throw complexity at you. If you decide to invest in the financial markets via an ETF (exchange-traded fund) – supposedly the 'simple' choice – you'll find that there are, in the UK, 1,647 different options. And should you be evaluating competing investments based on their APR, APY, CAGR or IRR? The investment industry seems to believe that you know and care what these abbreviations mean, but don't worry – few people do.

Ultimately, if your bucket sizes are wrong, none of this complexity matters anyway: you won't be satisfied with the outcome, because you'll either fall short of your dreams or be kept up at night by fear. And if your bucket sizes are right, no amount of studying comparison tables or trying to figure out what on earth a 'Sharpe ratio' is will result in a meaningful improvement.

The catch is that knowing what you truly want – and which painful trade-offs you're willing to accept to get it – is more mindbending than trying to calculate the equations that underlie Modern Portfolio Theory by hand. You won't get it exactly right, and your preferences and attitudes will change over time. But merely by trying, you cut through an incredible amount of noise and are vastly more likely to be satisfied with where you end up.

4

MYTH You should always aim to buy your own home: rising prices will make you rich, and renting is throwing money away.

REALITY A home offers you protection, but nothing more – and it's less of a one-way bet than it first seems.

CHAPTER 4
THE HOME-OWNERSHIP MYTH

If, like me, you live in Britain, there is one piece of financial advice that you will have heard more than any other. From practically the moment you start earning money in your first Sunday job, the importance of 'saving up for a house' is drilled into you. Buying your first home is considered a major life milestone – and, whether they admit it or not, most people see others as less successful if they're still 'stuck' renting. This obsession is backed up by an unusual level of agreement between all political parties: whoever is in power, an array of schemes and tax incentives exists both to help people 'get onto the ladder' and ensure they pay less tax when selling a home than any other asset.

It's not just Britain. Home ownership is a core element of the 'American Dream' (again, bolstered by various tax deductions), and schemes to support the aspiration of home ownership also exist in Canada, Australia and New Zealand. Even in countries like Germany and the Netherlands, which historically have a high proportion of renters and provide robust tenant protection, home ownership is becoming increasingly common.

For this reason, I've become accustomed to people looking at me a bit funny when I tell them that I don't own the home I live in. Their immediate assumption seems to be that I've either lost my mind or that I must secretly be living on the breadline. Their surprise isn't entirely unwarranted: I do host a show called *The Property Podcast* after all.

But while I might be chased to the airport with pitchforks for putting this in print, I'm not convinced that owning your home is anywhere near as important as it's made out to be – and for some people, it's actively the wrong thing to do. Of course, I'm not saying it's wrong for everyone: as we'll see, there are ample practical, emotional and financial reasons why it will be the right choice in many cases. My point is just that, despite all the endless advice to the contrary, buying your own home will not make you rich. In fact, as I mentioned in the previous chapter, it belongs in your Protect bucket: the protection it offers may be incredibly valuable, but what it isn't going to do is dramatically enhance your wealth in the same way other investments can.

This is not an easy myth to unpick, and I know I have my work cut out for me in this chapter. So let's begin by taking a few steps back and understanding more precisely what I mean by a Protect bucket in the first place.

THE UNIQUE PROTECTION OF CASH

Your Protect bucket is, basically, a rainy day fund. It will be there if you lose your job, if the economy unexpectedly collapses, or if ill-health prevents you from earning a living. Importantly, even if disaster doesn't strike, it still does its job by protecting you from lying awake with visions of some misfortune leaving you destitute.

Clearly, an important component of any Protect bucket is boring old cash. In fact, as anyone who's looked into personal finance for more than ten minutes will know, before you start investing you need to have carved out an 'emergency fund' that's held solely in cash. This fund will always make up the core of your Protect bucket, and deserves its place there due to two protective benefits that cash is unique in possessing. The first is that you can get your hands on it instantly: no need to find a buyer for your property, shares or other assets. This means you can use it to cover unexpected setbacks – a broken-down car, a dodgy boiler – within hours.

The second is that it has a 'face value' that is guaranteed at any given time. A dollar will always be a dollar, and a pound will always be a pound. Even if aliens invade – and the stock, bond and property markets all drop by 90 per cent in the ensuing panic – any cash you hold will be worth the same tomorrow as it is today.

Yet there's a problem: your £5 may be guaranteed to always be £5, but the amount of goods and services you can buy with that £5 falls over time due to inflation. In an ideal world, the interest you earn from keeping your cash in the bank would compensate for this. But, as we've seen, for almost the whole of the past fifteen years the rate of inflation has been higher than the rate of interest paid by the typical bank account. Result: you might put £100 into the bank and take £105 out at a later date, only to find that your £105 buys you less than your £100 would have done in the first place.

So while any cash you hold won't lose 'nominal' value under any circumstances, it's guaranteed to lose purchasing power over the years – and receiving interest on it may not be enough to compensate. In other words, the only way to avoid the risk of losing a lot of money is to accept the certainty of losing a bit of money. That was certainly true of any poor saver who set some money aside in March 2020, who would have watched their cash lose over 15 per cent of its value by 2024, even if they'd placed it in the most rewarding savings account available. And, as we saw in Chapter 1, this is likely to remain the case in the potentially inflationary years ahead.

With this dilemma in mind, how big should your emergency fund be? There are some simple rules of thumb, such as 'six months of living costs', which you can use to set a minimum level of cash you want to hold on to. But the right answer for you might be less than that or far more: it all depends on how you balance your desire for protection against the competing motivations of maintenance and improvement.

This becomes clear when you look at the finance habits of multi-millionaires, who don't realistically have the risk of running out of money unless they do something insanely stupid. If there was a 'right' answer, you'd expect them all to do the same thing – but, in reality, their behaviour differs dramatically. Take entrepreneur Noah Kagan, for example. He's spoken about how he keeps millions of dollars in cash, even though he knows full well he'll never need it and that it's losing value all the time. Despite this, he finds it reassuring to see a big number in his bank account – and the amount he earns from his other investments is still enough for him to become richer every year.

Others take the opposite approach. Shaan Puri – an investor and entrepreneur in a similar financial situation to Kagan – is deeply bothered by cash, because for him it represents a missed opportunity. He's painfully aware that it's earning almost nothing when it's sitting around, and investing it could turn it into far more cash – so he keeps his bank balance as low as possible.

Ultimately, whatever our level of wealth, we're all walking the same tightrope: trying to keep our Protect bucket full enough to keep us safe without forgoing investments that have the potential to make us money rather than losing it. To find the right balance and estimate the amount of cash to keep in your Protect bucket, I find it helps to tackle the practical and psychological aspects separately.

For the practical:

- Estimate your monthly essential living costs, such as food, rent and utilities: those that you wouldn't easily be able to cut back on in a pinch.

- Deduct any income sources that would continue even if you're not working – which may be investment income, insurance, state support or anything else.

- Multiply what remains by the number of months that you might, in a worst-case scenario, be unable to work for.

You now have your best estimate of how much cash you might realistically need. Importantly, this must be separate from any money you're building up for other purposes – like a deposit for a house. Your emergency fund should be what you'd fall back on if the worst happened without having to compromise your investment goals.

Now, looking at that number, how does it make you feel? This is where the psychological aspect comes in.

- Does it seem like too much? In that case, can you access an overdraft or reasonably priced debt if it came to it? Is there a family member you could move in with to cut costs, and would you genuinely be willing to do so?

- Or does it not seem like enough? Then go higher – but put any excess amount into its own dedicated account. This account represents money that you might choose to invest in the future if your preferences change, whereas the other is your 'true' emergency fund that can't otherwise be touched.

Just as with your overall bucket sizes, the amount of cash you want (and need) to hold back will change over time: this is something you'll need to continually re-assess rather than making a one-off decision. Counter-intuitively, I've found myself holding back more cash (both as an absolute amount and as a proportion) as my overall wealth has grown – probably because the swings in my investments can be uncomfortably large, making a healthy cash baseline more reassuring.

But there's a twist: many people will have a Protect bucket that's many multiples bigger as a proportion of their wealth than they think it is. And that's because your Protect bucket isn't just made up of cash. If you own a home, that belongs in there too.

WHY YOUR HOME WON'T MAKE YOU RICH

At first glance, your home appears to be the exact opposite of a cash emergency fund. It doesn't have a 'face value' that never changes, and it's about as illiquid as an investment can get. If you want to turn your house into cash, it'll take you months rather than minutes.

Clearly, though, as an asset it does have protective value. Indeed, one of the main motivations to buy a home is the control it gives you over your living situation: even when you have a mortgage, it still feels more secure than renting. Then, once the mortgage is paid off, no one can take your home away from you.

Purely protective, though? This is going to be a hard case for me to make. We all know people who've owned a home for 20+ years and seen an extra 'zero' added to the end of its value while they've been quietly living there and going about their business. Surely this is an exception to the rule that any asset can only serve a single motivation: doesn't a home protect our living situation while also improving our financial position over time?

I'm not convinced this has ever been true – and it's less true now than ever. Say you bought a home twenty years ago for £200,000, and now it's worth £500,000. Over that time you've also been chipping away at the mortgage, and now you own it outright. This has made you a lot wealthier, on paper. But what does it mean for you really?

The Home-Ownership Myth

Well, for a start, you spent twenty years saving money each month and directing those savings towards reducing the balance of your mortgage. If you hadn't had a mortgage, those savings could all have been directed towards investments in your Maintain or Improve buckets. As your mortgage balance shrank, the only effect was more protection: you moved steadily closer to the ultimate protection of owning it outright.

Now you do own it outright, there's great news: your initial investment has been multiplied many, many times over. You might have put in as little as £20,000 when you bought, and now if you sold it you'd have £500,000. At this point, can't that gain be translated into more Maintain- or Improve-style assets?

Well, here's the rub: only if you sold your home. Presumably you've chosen to live in your home because you like it, so if you sold it and bought somewhere else, you'd want to buy somewhere of an equivalent size, quality and location. That new home would, therefore, presumably cost roughly the same as your current one – so all your gains would be spent, and you'd be no further ahead.

So while it might seem like this extra protection is only temporary and can be converted into Maintain or Improve assets later, that's only true if you move to a smaller home or one in a cheaper area – leaving you with cash that you can then invest elsewhere. This is fine in theory, but something that people struggle to do in practice. In the UK, where owner-occupiers stay in the same home for an average of nearly seventeen years, 30 per cent of homes have two or more spare bedrooms. It's a similar story in much of the rich world.

Even if we assume that you do eventually downsize or move to a cheaper area, it doesn't change the fact that your home is purely protective during the time that you're living there. Similarly, you can remodel or improve your home to increase its value, but the only effect is more protection until you move out into a smaller or less desirable home. You sometimes hear people claiming when quizzed about their retirement that 'my property is my pension', but this is nonsensical: whether your home is worth £100,000 or £1 million, it's doing the same job for you – so it can only become 'your pension' if you're genuinely planning to move to somewhere significantly smaller or otherwise cheaper.

If you're still not willing to accept that your home offers nothing more than protection, I'll offer one concession. Work out the current value of an alternative home that you'd genuinely be willing to move to – whether specifically to further your investment goals, or for lifestyle reasons. Any difference between this and the value of your current home could be seen to represent a potential future contribution to your Maintain or Improve buckets that just happens to be sheltered in your Protect bucket for now. As we've seen, this isn't a move that people tend to make in practice. But if, for example, you're planning to relocate internationally in the future or you're itching to move somewhere smaller once you've got the kids out of the way, it might be true for you.

Don't get the wrong idea: I'm not saying that buying your own home is a bad investment. In many ways, it's a dream asset. It offers some protection against house prices going up faster than inflation, because your home and any equivalent homes you might want to buy in future will presumably be going up at a similar rate. In many parts of the world, the tax treatment is kinder than on any other asset too. And you truly are benefiting from very real, practical protection: by the time you own it outright, your need for shelter will be met for the rest of your life (except for taxes and maintenance), even if you don't generate any income.

But, nonetheless, it is purely protective – and the amount of that protection is capped at the cost of renting an equivalent home. But does this matter? After all, renting is commonly thought of as just throwing money away. Isn't owning a home unambiguously good because, by paying your own mortgage, it saves you from being stuck paying off someone else's?

RENTING IS NOT 'MONEY DOWN THE DRAIN'

An unfortunate reality of life is that, whatever you do, you can't get away from housing costs. You'll always have repairs and maintenance. You'll always have taxes. And less obviously, you'll always have opportunity cost: that is, what your money could be earning if you'd put it somewhere other than into buying a home.

Say you put down a deposit of £20,000 to buy a home. That's undoubtedly an investment, but it comes with an opportunity cost: if you hadn't used it to buy a home, it could be invested in somewhere like the stock market, potentially growing in value and earning dividends.

Then there's your monthly mortgage payment. Each payment you make is generally made up of two components: part of it is a repayment that reduces what you owe, and part of it is paying the interest that represents the cost of borrowing the money in the first place.

The interest component is no different from rent: it's a cost you're paying to live in your home without having paid to own it outright. Instead of renting the home from a landlord, you're renting the money you used to buy the home from a bank.

The part that's being used to pay down the mortgage might seem like it's purely to your benefit: a repayment of £100 reduces the mortgage and increases your equity in the home by the same amount. Yet there's an opportunity cost lurking here too: every £100 invested in your home also represents £100 that can't go towards other investment assets that could grow in value and pay you an income.

As time goes on, that opportunity cost grows. By the time your house is worth £1 million, your opportunity cost is gigantic: there's a huge amount of money trapped in your home (offering you no more benefit than it did when your home was worth £100,000), and it can't be invested elsewhere.

Even if we disregard the opportunity cost, renting can still work out to be cheaper than buying. Between 2011 and 2020, buying the typical US home with a mortgage was 12 per cent cheaper than renting it. But that was at a time when mortgage rates were at historic lows. Now, according to an analysis by *The Economist*, it's cheaper to rent than to own in 89 per cent of US counties. That doesn't factor in the equity that owners are building in their homes but nor does it account for opportunity cost. If renters were to take the equivalent down payment and invest it into another asset that at least matches the performance of the housing market, they'd be better off.

In reality, though, most renters aren't in a position to do this. In the UK, only 54 per cent of renters have any level of savings, compared to 71 per cent of those who own with a mortgage and 86 per cent of those who own outright; meanwhile, the median net worth of the typical US renter is $6,300, while the median net worth of the typical US homeowner is $255,000. There are multiple reasons for this, including that homeowners tend to be older so have had more time to build wealth, and the fact they could afford a down payment suggests they were in a more secure financial position to start with. But regardless of the reason, this stark difference goes a long way towards explaining why people often blindly assume that owning is always better: they see owners who are well-off and renters who aren't, and assume that it's the ownership that makes the difference. Yet if a renter started with the same amount of capital as a homeowner and chose to invest it elsewhere, a significant part of the difference would disappear.

There's another reason that ownership is assumed to always

be superior: the people raving about the importance of 'getting on the housing ladder' have personally benefited enormously from owning their homes. But that might be because, unbeknownst to them, they've been living through a highly unusual period in world history.

THE END OF 'RUNAWAY HOUSE PRICES'

It's hardly surprising that people tend to see their home as a major engine of wealth-creation given that house prices in many parts of the world have grown rapidly over the past few decades. This has given rise to a widespread perception that property 'always goes up in value': you can't go wrong with it, people argue, and, indeed, you should do everything you can to jump on the ladder before prices get further out of your reach.

But if you stop and think about it for a minute, why would that be the case? Houses don't become more expensive to build over time: if anything, new technology should enable better quality cheaper. Is it that there's ever more demand for housing due to an increasing population, and reasons like NIMBYism are preventing supply from matching it? This is somewhat true, but if you look at house price trends in the US and UK, they bear virtually no relation to how quickly or slowly the population is growing at the time.

Conversely, you can see why the shares of companies would go up in value: they learn to sell products more cheaply and efficiently over time. You can even see why largely unproductive assets, like gold and Bitcoin, would go up in value: there's a genuine cap in supply, so any increase in demand will raise the price. But houses? None of these reasons apply. And as it turns out, over long stretches of time, they haven't gone up in value after all. Or, at least, they haven't after factoring in inflation.

If you'd bought a house in the US in 1890, twenty-five years later it would have increased in value by less than the rate of inflation – meaning that, if you could have kept your money in a bank account that paid an inflation-matching rate of interest, you would have been better off than if you'd bought a house. Same story if you'd bought in 1920: by 1945, you'd be no better off in inflation-adjusted terms. And the same again if you'd bought in 1950: you'd be slightly down by 1975.

Even between 1970 and 1995, inflation-adjusted house prices didn't budge. This initially seems hard to believe because nominal house prices rocketed: a typical family home that would have cost $23,000 in 1970 was worth $130,000 by 1995. Yet when you dig into the data, you find that 100 per cent of this gain was due to inflation.

But then something changed: for the twenty-five-year period from 1995 until 2020, even after stripping out the effect of inflation, house prices increased by 60 per cent. Then they kept going, reaching 100 per cent by 2022. It was a similar story in the UK: from 1975 until 1995, house prices after removing the effect of inflation were almost completely flat. Between 1995 and 2020, they increased by an astonishing 116 per cent.

House prices exploding in value like this feels normal to us because it's what we've all lived through recently – but, historically, it's extremely unusual. So what changed?

In short: a long-term downward trend in interest rates. As we entered the 1990s, the US interest rate was 8.25 per cent. By the time we entered the 2000s, it was 5.5 per cent. By the time we entered the 2010s, it was at 0.25 per cent. The pattern in the UK was the same: indeed, in the early 1990s rates briefly spiked up to 15 per cent. By the turn of the millennium, they'd fallen to 5.5 per cent, and by 2020 had reached an all-time low of 0.1 per cent. One of the most basic concepts in the whole of economics is that as interest rates fall, asset prices rise: when it's cheaper to borrow money, more people are willing and able to buy assets, which pushes up their price. In the case of homes, lower mortgage payments mean you can afford a bigger loan – and sellers know this, so prices tend to increase.

So anyone you know who has seen the value of their home soar since the 1990s (or, for some, since the 1970s) has benefited from two effects. One is a highly unusual multi-decade fall in interest rates, which gave house prices an enormous boost even after accounting for inflation. Interest rates have, of course, adjusted upwards since their historic 2020 low, so there is the potential for them to fall again and give asset prices another boost. But another shift of that magnitude and that duration? You wouldn't want to bet on it. It seems more likely that this was a once-in-a-century anomaly, which persisted for so long that it ended up feeling normal.

The other effect is simply inflation: a home costs more today than it did twenty years ago, but the same is true for a carton of milk. Yet, unlike milk, you tend to buy a home using debt – in the form of a mortgage. This means that rather than just being a variable that needs correcting for, inflation is an absolute gift for homeowners.

Take someone in the UK who bought a home in 1975 and held onto it until 1995: a period when, as we've seen, in inflation-adjusted terms it virtually didn't increase in price at all. But the nominal price – the price they could expect to sell it for – increased by 391 per cent. In other words, a £100,000 home would end up being worth a whisker under £500,000.

But here's the magic: imagine you bought the property with £25,000 of your own cash, and a mortgage for the remaining £75,000. You also managed to negotiate terms where you only had to pay the interest, without paying down the balance of the loan at all. After twenty-five years, your £75,000 loan would still be a £75,000 loan. But that £25,000 equity that you put in would have ballooned to £425,000.

This is the main reason that I'm so enthusiastic about property investment: you can borrow a large amount of money which always remains static as long as you pay the interest, and use it to buy an asset that typically rises in value at least along with inflation over the long term. Not only that, but you get to collect rental income along the way.

Remember, though: this is only the case for investment property, which (as we'll see later) you'd hold in your Improve bucket if you were using a mortgage. Although your own home benefits from the same effect, that inflation-related increase in value is of no practical benefit until you sell it to buy somewhere smaller or cheaper.

So given that runaway house prices are an historical anomaly driven by a trend that's now reversed, and general inflation-linked growth in house prices is only beneficial for investment property (until you're ready to make a major lifestyle change), we come to the big question: should you have a home in your Protect bucket at all?

SHOULD YOU BUY YOUR OWN HOME?

Just because owning a home over the past few decades may have been an unusually good deal, that doesn't mean it's bad at other times. On top of the financial advantages, it has practical and emotional ones too. In many countries renters lack security, you can't even paint a wall without permission, and there's that feeling of somewhere being 'yours' that's hard to put a monetary value on.

But still, in much of the world financial success is equated with owning a home to an unhelpful extent. There are plenty of life situations where it can make sense to remain a renter for longer, which largely boil down to a need for flexibility over stability.

For example, many younger people would benefit from the

The Home-Ownership Myth

ability to move to pursue new career opportunities – but with it taking at least a few months to sell a house, ownership ties you to a geographical area and limits your options. The same goes for times when your family situation isn't settled: if you bought a small apartment then three years later wanted to move into a larger place with a partner to start a family, the transaction costs would be enormous. As a general rule, buying a home rather than renting it only makes sense if you know for sure that you'll want to live there for at least five years – probably more like ten – which allows the impact of the upfront transaction costs to be spread out over multiple years.

If you do want stability and know you'll be somewhere for the long term, buying might make practical sense. But now we're living in a time when it's harder than ever for the average person to save anything at all, it still brings uncomfortable trade-offs. If you could put yourself in the position to benefit from the protection of home ownership while still filling your other buckets, you would – but this is tough to do. In practice, many people have nothing left over after paying their mortgage, meaning that they're gradually accumulating more and more protection but little of anything else.

There's a further drawback to being in the position of 'aspiring homeowner', which is that while you're saving up your deposit you need to keep it in cash. As we've seen, that's the only way you can be sure of its value at the point that you need it. And while you're allocating your savings to cash in your Protect bucket (which will later convert into home equity, still in your Protect bucket), that cash can't be used to build up investments in the more rewarding Maintain and Improve buckets. If it takes you five years to save up, that's five years during which your savings are keeping pace with inflation at best – and missing out on the long-term gains you'd see if you'd been dripping them into other investments, like the stock market.

There's no easy answer to the 'buy or rent' question: when it comes to your home, there's such an intertwined set of personal and financial considerations that, even with perfect foresight and the world's most complex financial model, it would be impossible to know for sure what will be the right move. Obviously I can't know what's best for you, and I'm not trying to steer you away from home ownership – I'm just encouraging you to explore the question, rather than buying into the myth that owning a home is always the right choice and you can rely on it to make you wealthy.

The implications of all this are threefold. First, don't blindly assume that buying a home as early as possible is always desirable. Anyone who tells you that it is probably doesn't realise that they're basing their belief on a brief and highly unusual period of history. Second, there's no rush: people often feel a need to 'get on the ladder' because they see prices always going up, and worry about them drifting further out of reach. But, most of the time, they're only going up in line with inflation – so if your savings and wages are at least close to keeping up, you're not really falling any further behind.

And third, ideally don't throw so much at buying the most expensive home you can afford as early as possible that you can't contribute to any other investments at all. There's a good chance that owning a home will ultimately be the right decision for you, but you might prefer to introduce some balance by filling your Maintain and Improve buckets at the same time – even if it pushes home ownership back by a few years.

After all, everyone knows that it's critical to start making investments early because the compounding effect over time is so powerful. Or is it?

5

MYTH Compounding returns are the eighth wonder of the world: they will turn even small investments into serious wealth.

REALITY Future returns may disappoint you, and progress takes decades – so put the basics on autopilot, then look for bigger wins.

CHAPTER 5

THE COMPOUNDING MYTH

Take a grain of rice. Double it, so you have two. Double that, so you have four. Now keep doubling another sixty-one times. How many grains of rice do you have?

The answer, in good news for anyone who fancies a risotto, is more than eighteen quintillion.

Or take a sheet of paper and somehow (with superhuman strength) fold it in half forty-two times. How high is your stack? You'll have guessed from how I've framed the question that it's going to be a surprisingly big answer – but you'll probably still be shocked to learn that it would be thick enough to reach the moon.

This is all great pub trivia, but what does it have to do with money? Well, you won't find a non-Ponzi investment that routinely doubles your money every year like the grains of rice, but the logic is the same. You start with £100, and earn, say, a 5 per cent return each year. In the first year, this nets you £5. Then the next year you earn 5 per cent on your £105, which means you're handed £5.25. And so on. Live long enough, and you end up sucking in all the money in the universe and your wallet develops its own gravitational pull. Or, more prosaically, investing £500 per month for thirty years means you end up with £416,000 (assuming a 5 per cent return), of which more than half comes from compounding rather than your own contributions.

As a result, a generation of investors has been told that, in the long term, the key to a prosperous life is simple: exponential compounding. The acclaimed investing book *The Little Book of*

Common Sense Investing (2007) by John C. Bogle says, 'By owning a broadly diversified portfolio of stocks and holding it over the long term, compounding works its magic, turning even modest investments into substantial wealth.' *Your Money or Your Life* (1992) by Vicki Robin and Joe Dominguez has a similar theme: 'Investing your money wisely so it earns a steady return and compounds over time is the surest way to financial independence.' Popular investment platform Nutmeg refers to it as a 'miracle', and even Albert Einstein is widely quoted as having said that it was the eighth wonder of the world (but there's no evidence that he really did).

It's true that compounding is a powerful force, but its ability to transform your financial life has been dangerously oversold. Reading this advice, you're left with the impression that all you need to maintain your current lifestyle later in life is to invest regularly in basic financial assets – and that, provided you've started investing early enough, the miracle of compounding will take care of your future.

Think again. While compounding will certainly be critical to the long-term results delivered by your Maintain bucket, having too much faith in it could leave you extremely disappointed, and without enough time to do anything about it.

WHY COMPOUNDING WON'T SAVE YOU

If you're looking forward to whiling away the last few decades of your life on luxury cruises and spending long afternoons on the golf course, don't under any circumstances google anything related to pensions – where the current situation has been variously described as a 'ski-slope of doom' and a 'slow-motion car crash'.

It wasn't always this way. As we saw in Chapter 2, it was once the norm for workers to look forward to retiring with a

The Compounding Myth

guaranteed income every year for life, based on their final salary and the number of years they'd worked. Put in a standard forty-year career, and they could sail off around the Caribbean with the same annual income they achieved at their earnings peak without the slightest worry about whether they'd saved enough or what the markets were going to do next. But, today, virtually every scheme like this has closed to new members. If you want to maintain the life you have now without having to work, you'll need another approach.

The conventional way to go about this is to make investments earlier in life in the hope that they eventually grow into a healthy fund by the time you need them. For most people, this involves filling their Maintain bucket: buying a collection of investments that will compound in value over time, allowing them to enjoy the same lifestyle in retirement that they have today.

The task is a daunting one for two reasons. Firstly, there's the responsibility of choosing for yourself what you should be investing in. Somehow you, with no particular expertise in the matter, have to pick a collection of assets that will allow you to achieve your goal. And it's hardly like the stakes are low: if you fail in your role as an amateur fund manager, the price is that you'll run out of money to live on. Luckily, avoiding this fate isn't as difficult as it first appears, although the ideal recipe has changed. (We'll cover this in the next chapter.)

And, secondly, there's the sheer amount you need to accumulate. Let's say you're not yet convinced that breaking the time–money connection is for you, and you want to err on the safe side by having enough accumulated by the time you're sixty-seven to see you through the rest of your life with what the Pension and Lifetime Savings Association defines as a 'comfortable' retirement income of £43,100. Plugging this into a retirement calculator reveals that for someone in the UK who qualifies for the full level of state support, this would require a pension pot of more than £650,000. Anyone with higher aspirations, or who lives in a country with lower levels of state assistance, would need to build up far, far more. How on earth are you supposed to save anything like that amount while also buying a house, potentially raising kids, and generally having a life worth living?

Faced with such a seemingly impossible task, it's tempting to chuck in the metaphorical towel, focus on living for today, and push aside the thought of how you'll navigate your later years. So, to provide enough hope to motivate people into action rather than give up completely, a new investing religion sprang up: the religion of compounding returns.

As luck would have it, the last few decades have been kind to compounders. As we explored in Chapter 1, the long-term structural decline in interest rates benefited stocks, bonds and real estate simultaneously. This resulted in a strong growth rate for most investment portfolios, allowing compounding to work its magic more quickly. At the same time, inflation was barely even thought about for decades: central bankers spoke of a 'great moderation' where their clever manipulations of monetary levers had banished it for ever. The result? Your assets were compounding quickly, and you could be confident that inflation wouldn't take too big a bite out of your future living standards.

But that's all changed, and the cracks in the cult of compounding are showing. As we've seen, the future is likely to be defined by volatile bouts of inflation, perhaps averaging out at a level that's higher than the rate of interest. This spells trouble for anyone assuming their investments will grow in value as consistently as they have done in the past.

Higher inflation alone would be bad enough: that £650,000 figure assumes a 2.5 per cent average rate of inflation. If inflation ends up higher still, then the sum will need to be significantly larger just to keep up.

The Compounding Myth

Meanwhile, the end of 'free money' makes things even trickier: now interest rates are no longer on a constant decline, there's no structural force pushing up the valuation of everything at the same time. It's impossible to say with certainty, but it seems highly likely that the general rate of return on most investments is going to be lower over the next two decades than it has been over the past two.

You wouldn't necessarily be aware of any of this from listening to the new generation of financial influencers who have come to prominence since around 2020, and whose insights have not all been wildly helpful. Suddenly, rather than a sober conversation with a professional, ever more people are having their views of investment shaped by influential accounts on TikTok and Instagram. Improbable as it sounds, videos explaining the concept of compounding returns have racked up tens of millions of views.

How can a higher awareness of the power of investing be a bad thing? The problem is that many of these influencers are compensated when someone signs up for an investment account. This means that to prompt people into action so they get paid, it's in their interest to make the gains from investing sound as exciting as possible. As a result, these influencers locked onto the (true) fact that the US stock market has made an average annual return of around 10 per cent over the past 100 years, and have used this as a justification to demonstrate the eye-popping wealth you could end up with by simply investing and seeing your money compound at a rate of 10 per cent per year.

Much as I hate to risk denting anyone's enthusiasm for investing, there's a series of dangerous holes in this logic. For a start, history tells us it's almost unheard of for one country to lead the way for century after century. If the US isn't going to continue to be the big global winner over the duration of your investing lifespan, are you confident you'll be able to pick the new winner in advance and put your money there instead? And even if you could, would you be comfortable with putting all your eggs in that basket, knowing that stock markets tend to crash (defined as a decline of more than 30 per cent) once every twelve years?

Let's say you're not, so you diversify – meaning you spread your eggs between several different baskets. By definition, they won't all be the best all the time – so by giving up on the risky dream of picking the single big winner, you may be settling for a 7 per cent rather than a 10 per cent return.

It gets worse from there, because the 10 per cent figure didn't account for inflation, and nor does the 7 per cent we've reluctantly downgraded ourselves to. Some of those returns are merely enabling you to stand still: if inflation runs at 2 per cent per year, in 'real terms' (meaning after stripping out inflation and allowing us to think in today's money) we're only making a 5 per cent annual return.

I'd still consider these assumptions optimistic, but I don't want to depress you further – because the difference between compounding at a theoretical 10 per cent versus a more realistic 5 per cent is massive. If you started with £100,000 and compounded it at 10 per cent for thirty years, you'd end up with a fraction under £2 million. So, compounding at a rate of 5 per cent, would it be half of that: £1 million? No: because of the way compounding works, you'd only end up with £500,000.

With the combined effect of a changing financial world and setting out with more realistic assumptions, compounding starts looking distinctly less magical. Unfortunately, though, that's not where its drawbacks end.

MIRACLES TAKE TIME

Let's say that, at the age of twenty, you're earning £30,000 and you follow the typical advice to invest 10 per cent of your salary.

The Compounding Myth

Each year, your salary increases by 5 per cent, so you diligently increase the amount you save by 5 per cent too.

Your investments also earn you returns of 5 per cent per year. And to keep it simple, we'll imagine that this 5 per cent return is after factoring in inflation – so whenever we look at sums of money you receive in the future, they'll be able to buy you the same amount of stuff as they would today.

In the first year you put in £3,000, and earn returns of £150. Big deal. But by the time you turn sixty, something incredible has happened: your investments are producing a return of £40,000 per year. All in all, your £3,000 investment pot has grown to £844,252 – of which you put in less than half, and the majority came from your investment returns.

This sounds like an incredible outcome: every year your money now earns more than your initial salary without any effort on your part. And all based on a very modest level of contributions.

So, by the time you're sixty years old, all is great. But let's check in on where you'd be at the halfway mark of forty years old, after diligently executing this plan for twenty years.

At this point, you're contributing £7,580 per year based on a £150,000 salary, and earning £7,484 in investment returns. If you stopped at this point, nothing that special would have happened at all: you'd have a total investment pot of £161,359, of which more than £102,000 – two-thirds – was money you put in yourself. If you decided after twenty years that corporate life wasn't for you, or you were forced to stop working due to illness or family commitments, that £7,484 of investment income wouldn't go far towards making up for your lack of earnings.

Similarly, what if you hadn't started at the age of twenty, and didn't make your first investment until you were forty instead? That's a common scenario, given that many people start earning later, or have debt to repay, or are busy building up their Protect bucket by saving for a house, or just have more exciting things to do with their spare time than learn about personal finance, so they never think to get started. Well, the good news is that you'd be starting with a higher salary so might be able to put more aside, but you'd still only have that same twenty years to work with – which, as we've seen, is barely enough for compounding to get going.

These examples demonstrate the unfortunate reality of compounding: it's all back-loaded. For the first couple of decades, the vast majority of the growth in your investment pile is coming from your own contributions, and it's only later that the 'returns on returns' start building up in a meaningful way. Astonishingly, in our twenty-to-sixty example, a full quarter of the investment pot ended up being accumulated in the last five years alone. This is why Warren Buffett made 99 per cent of his wealth after he turned sixty-five: it had already been compounding for forty years by then, and went on to compound for nearly thirty more. If you want to get seriously wealthy from compounding, you'd better be taking your vitamins.

So even if you start investing straight out of school, you won't notice the results until you're fifty or older. During the time in your life when you're most able to enjoy experiences that cost money and when your finances are the most stretched if you're raising a family, the money compounding away in the background is of no use at all. Then, just as you reach the age when your spending typically drops off – the house is paid off, the kids have left, and you're less motivated by the type of activities that cost a lot – your investments suddenly wake up and start making you wealthier and wealthier with every passing year. This is why it's common for people to die leaving huge inheritances behind, but without having had much in the way of experiences or material comforts during their own life; by the time the money was there, they couldn't get into the habit of spending it.

The Compounding Myth

This is the big limitation of much personal finance advice. It won't allow for anything more racy than consistent compounding – which means that, unless you're starting weirdly early, there isn't much time for the returns-on-returns effect to get going. If you've set your sights on more than mere comfort in retirement – you have the desire to build up a stonking pile of wealth that places nothing off-limits and leaves your family secure for generations to come – well, that's off the table too.

My aim in tearing down compounding isn't to depress you (even though I probably have done), and I don't mean to imply that it's pointless. You should absolutely take advantage of it, but you should also be realistic about what it's likely to achieve so you don't end up disappointed when it fails to deliver life-changing returns. By being clear-eyed about the limits of compounding now, you still have time to add other types of investment into the mix if you want to (which we'll cover in Chapter 7).

THE WIRING OF A COMPOUNDING MACHINE

Just because compounding isn't some magical mathematical secret that will solve all your problems doesn't mean we should throw it out entirely – but it does inform how we should go about using it. Compounding belongs squarely in the Maintain bucket: it can help you sustain your existing quality of life but is unlikely to transform it. That's not to be sniffed at: used effectively, compounding will allow 'good' to happen quietly in the background while you actively work on 'great'.

So, you should restrict the amount of conscious effort you dedicate to the compounding process. Depending on how you balance the three investment motivations of protection, maintenance and improvement, your Maintain bucket might make up the lion's share of your investments or just a sliver. But regardless of size, harnessing the benefits of exponential returns (without assigning it more importance than it deserves) involves building a compounding machine – a process that has four characteristics.

Effortless

The first characteristic of our compounding machine is that it should be *effortless* to operate.

As we've already covered, it might be realistic to achieve a return of 5 per cent above inflation without investing any time or developing any specialist knowledge. But let's imagine you're not willing to settle for that, so you spend your evenings and weekends reading books, watching investment YouTubers, learning how to read a balance sheet, digging into company reports and tracking competing theories about the future path of the economy. As a result, you boost the return you achieve from 5 per cent to 7 per cent.

That doesn't sound like much, but out-performing the average by 2 per cent every year is seriously difficult and most professionals don't manage it. Let's assume you pull it off, though. After twenty years (using the same assumptions as our example earlier), instead of having an investment pot of £161,000, you'd end up with . . . £198,500.

Even though I was using this example to make a point, I was so shocked that I had to re-run the numbers twice to check that it was true. But it is. Going from a 5 per cent annual investment return to a 7 per cent return earns you an extra £37,500 – in total, over twenty years. Even if you only spent two hours per week achieving this – which I think would be astonishingly low – your equivalent hourly rate to generate that excess over twenty years would be £9.37.

You could earn more than that by applying your time to pretty much anything else: you'd come out ahead by cleaning houses or driving an Uber, with none of the risk that your investments wouldn't out-perform. You could even sack the whole endeavour off and just use those extra hours to have fun and it wouldn't make all that much difference. This approach might even be safer, because when you try to beat the average there's a not insignificant chance that you'll end up making bad decisions and performing worse – meaning that every hour you spend is actually *costing* you money.

This is why your compounding needs to be effortless: it's just not worth making it effortful. Does this sound a bit fatalistic, like there's nothing you can do to positively influence your financial future? Don't worry: that's not the case at all. When we come to discuss your Improve bucket, we'll cover plenty of areas where you can apply some skill and effort (and accept some risk) to earn a much higher return. And as we covered when we were squashing the retirement lie, a far better use of those hours of research would be applying them to giving your career a boost. This would, without any risk whatsoever, result in your extra earnings vastly eclipsing the meagre increase in investment returns.

Consistent

The second principle is that it must be *consistent*.

We know that compounding works its magic over time, relying on a long and steady process of making small gains and reinvesting them. You can think of it like turning a giant, heavy handle: at first it's painful to even get it moving a tiny bit, but eventually you build up momentum until the handle is flying around so fast it's hard to stop. Yet if you kept stopping the handle just as it was getting going, you'd never reach that point: you'd be doing the exhausting early stages again and again, working up a sweat with little to show for it.

This is why, according to Warren Buffett's brilliant business partner Charlie Munger, 'the first rule of compounding is not to interrupt it unnecessarily'. It's far better to have a plan that you can steadily execute year in, year out than it is to be sporadically brilliant.

Automated

A popular online brokerage set out to identify what set their top performing clients apart from the rest, and discovered that they had an unexpected edge: they were dead. This rendered them immune to the temptation to meddle, leaving them (or more accurately their heirs, I suppose) better off than those who could still log on and hit 'buy' or 'sell' at what turned out to be the worst possible times.

This is why our compounding machine also needs to be *automated*: to protect us from ourselves.

To keep the examples in this chapter simple, I've been implying that our returns will be the same steady percentage every year. In fact, the one thing we know for sure is that this won't be the case. Some years will be fantastic – seeing returns of 15 per cent or more. Others will be dreadful: returns will be negative, so despite feeding the machine with more cash we'll end the year with less than we started.

Human psychology being what it is, if you adopt any approach other than consistently doing the exact same thing regardless of what's happening out in the world, you'll make mistakes that will irreversibly damage your wealth. It's unbelievably tempting to hold off from putting in this month's contribution because there are some scary stories in the news and the market is looking a bit wobbly: surely by waiting a bit, you'll be able to buy in at a lower price? But this will guide you towards doing exactly the wrong thing: buying only when sentiment is good and prices are higher, and holding off from buying when it's poor and the market is on sale.

Diversified

We've already seen that if you have the option of just accepting the average, it quite literally isn't worth your time to try to improve on it. At best you'll likely find yourself working for less than the minimum wage, and at worst you'll make the wrong decisions and end up worse off than if you hadn't bothered. Ensuring that your investments are *diversified* – just a fancy word for 'spreading your bets' – is how you achieve this attractive average.

But how diversified do you need to be? Is it just a case of buying into a tracker fund that aims to match the performance of the overall market and being done with it? Well, that steers us dangerously close to another myth, which we'll need to spend the whole of the next chapter unpicking.

HOW TO BUILD YOUR COMPOUNDING MACHINE

A well-oiled compounding machine starts with that classic piece of personal finance advice: 'pay yourself first'.

At its simplest, this just means setting up a regular transfer so money leaves your bank account as soon as you're paid, and is whisked away to your chosen investment platform. This ticks the boxes for automation, consistency and lack of effort: once set up, it becomes more effort to stop yourself from investing than to steadily continue. Alternatively, you might be able to have a regular investment taken directly from your salary as a pension contribution and matched up to a certain level by your employer. If this is on offer, it's free money and represents the highest return on investment you'll ever effortlessly achieve – with the only disadvantage being that it's locked away until you reach your country's pension age. This isn't a problem for most people, though, because we know that the Maintain bucket is something that only works if left to its own devices for decades anyway.

Your next move is to set up recurring monthly 'buys' of your chosen assets on your investment platform. Almost any platform will allow you to automate this process by choosing a list of investments you want to buy into, and allocating either a fixed amount of cash or a certain percentage of your cash deposit into each of them. This extra level of automation is important because otherwise your machine relies on you logging in and making investments each month. If you're like most people, this isn't something you can be trusted to do. The temptation to leave the cash sitting there while you 'wait and see' how the economic worry of the day plays out will be too strong – and inevitably, as soon as that worry is forgotten, a new one will come along. Result: you've saved (which is better than not saving), but will never manage to consistently invest.

The next step is a deceptively difficult one: do nothing. Now you've automated the process you don't need to log in – so do whatever it takes to hold yourself back from doing so. When you check how your investments have performed, you'll be tempted to interfere – and again, this is likely to damage your returns rather than enhance them (remember those deceased investment wizards?).

If necessary, hand over your password to someone you trust. At a minimum, whatever you do, don't install your broker's mobile app: the easier it is to check on your progress, the more you're at risk of messing things up. Even if you're fully aware that you're playing a game that's won over decades, seeing a sea of red numbers and downward arrows – which will sometimes be the case – isn't pleasant. Not only will it make you want to do

The Compounding Myth

ill-advised things, it's also not psychologically healthy. So automate, then stay away.

With your compounding machine humming along in the background, your Maintain bucket will steadily grow. It won't miraculously change your life, and you won't see the results any time soon, but you will become slightly better off in most years and see your wealth build. Your money will be earning progressively more money on your behalf, allowing you to eventually ease off on your own efforts.

You may have noticed, though, that I've glossed over a rather important detail: when you're setting up those automated investments, what should you be investing in? That question is so important it deserves a whole chapter of its own, especially as there's another particularly pernicious myth that we need to debunk.

6

MYTH Diversifying between stocks and bonds is the way to stay safe.

REALITY The old-school approach to diversification is no longer enough – today, you need to look much further.

CHAPTER 6
THE DIVERSIFICATION MYTH

2022 was the year that conventional financial wisdom failed.

It wasn't a vintage year for investors: those holding 100 per cent of their investment in stocks (using investment platform Vanguard's flagship LifeStrategy fund) saw their portfolios drop in value by 6 per cent. But that wasn't particularly unusual: we know the market has bad years every so often, and they could hardly complain given that it had increased by 19 per cent the previous year.

The shock was what happened to investors who had taken active measures to avoid such slumps. This group had chosen to dial down their risk by buying into a different version of the same fund that blended 60 per cent stocks with 40 per cent bonds. In every previous downturn, that choice would have been vindicated – but not this time. In fact, they fared even worse: their investments ended the year down by more than 11 per cent.

This experience ran counter to one of the core assumptions that has driven how financial professionals have put together slow-and-steady, low-risk portfolios for the last 70+ years. As Burton G. Malkiel's classic book *A Random Walk Down Wall Street* (1973) put it: 'A mixed portfolio of stocks and bonds can be less risky than either component taken by itself. Diversification is a time-honored method of reducing risk.' But not in 2022. As one disappointed diversifier wrote at the time, 'I'm scared to look at my balances. I'd probably start crying.'

So what went wrong? Was 2022 just a one-off blip that we can ignore and move on from? Well, while we can hope to go a long time without seeing an exact repeat of that year, it exposed the possibility that even the most cautious investors are taking on more risk than they might realise. For anyone who wants to build a Maintain bucket that will survive whatever's thrown at it for several decades, this has major implications.

WHY INDEX FUNDS AREN'T ENOUGH

Much like the perils of smoking and the benefits of wearing a seatbelt, these days you barely need to explain that trying to pick individual stocks is not a wise idea. Sure, the temptation to pick the next Nvidia (which recently more than doubled in value in less than six months) is always there – but, deep down, most people know that there's far too high a risk that you inadvertently pick the next WeWork (down from more than $500 a share to mere pennies in less than two years).

Indeed, look up any 'investing for beginners' video on YouTube and it will evangelise about the merits of investing in index funds. A 'fund' is just a pooled investment: everyone puts money in, and that money is invested in the shares of a selection of different companies. An 'index' is a grouping of companies that meet some kind of criteria, such as the 500 biggest companies in the US (the S&P 500 index) or the 100 biggest companies in the UK (the FTSE 100).

An index fund, then, simply pools investors' money and invests it in all the companies that fall within a certain index. The result for each investor is that they earn the same returns as they would have done by buying each company individually, without all the hassle and transaction costs. And because the fund is only aiming to mirror the performance of an index rather than to beat it, the whole thing can be set up to run on autopilot. This means that fund management fees, which eat up a big chunk of investors' returns when there's a team of

The Diversification Myth

stockpickers trying to make clever decisions, are so low as to almost be irrelevant.

Very neat, and worth all the evangelising. Index funds avoid the risky business of trying to pick individual winners, instead averaging out the Nvidias and the WeWorks. You won't double your money within a year, but nor are you likely to lose a substantial proportion of it: there will be both winners and losers within the index, meaning the extremes will cancel each other out and leave you with a steadier ride. And it doesn't require any effort or knowledge: you'd struggle to know how any given company is likely to perform over the next twenty years, but you can be pretty sure that on average the companies across a country will become more valuable. By owning an index fund, you reap the rewards when they do.

This is a perfect example of the principle of diversification. You benefit from diversification whenever you hold several different assets, as long as they don't have too much in common with each other. If you owned shares in ten different oil companies, for example, you'd expect them all to be affected in the same way by a drop in global demand, so there's minimal diversification benefit.

Index funds are more diversified – although, critically, not to quite the extent it first appears. They clearly avoid the problem of the oil companies example, because they're made up of banks, tech companies, retailers and plenty else besides – each of which you'd expect to perform well under slightly different conditions, at different times. Yet if you buy into an index fund that limits its investments to a particular country, diversification might not get you as far as you'd expect. After all, if you were patting yourself on the back for investing in an S&P 500 fund at the start of 2022 rather than succumbing to the temptation of trying to pick a winner, the loss of nearly 20 per cent that you'd have experienced by Christmas would have left you wondering what was so safe about it. The same dissatisfaction would have been felt by long-term investors in the UK's FTSE 100, who watched in frustration as it took sixteen years to beat the level it achieved on the last day of the twentieth century.

Clearly, the problem here is that if something happens to affect the fortunes of the country that those companies are headquartered in, it tends to hit the valuations of all those companies at the same time. To sidestep this, you need to go a level deeper and build in some geographical diversification – which, happily, can also be achieved within a fund. It's just as easy to buy into a world index, which invests in individual funds that focus on different countries. Each of those funds contains hundreds of individual companies within their target country – so with a few taps on a broker's app, you can be exposed to the average performance of thousands of companies in countries from Spain to South Korea.

The bad news for anyone wanting a steady and predictable Maintain bucket, though, is that even this international approach doesn't provide you with the same diversification benefit that it used to. Over the past century, the US market has come to dominate the world. Enthusiastic investors have driven up the valuations of American companies to the point where they now account for over 60 per cent of the total market value of all companies worldwide. As a result, a fund that tracks a US index will also make up at least 60 per cent of a typical global index fund. iShares' world tracker, which is one of the biggest, holds shares in 1,435 different companies – but 71 per cent of its total exposure is to the US. The consequence is simple: if America has a bad year, everyone has a bad year.

And there's another danger lurking for diversifiers: within the all-powerful US market, a handful of tech giants have outsized influence. Between them, Apple, Nvidia, Microsoft, Amazon and Meta account for more than a quarter of the entire US market's value. An investor in a global fund might then have exposure to the combined fortunes of thousands of companies around the world, but the reality is that if a handful of companies in Silicon Valley have a tough time, they'll be disproportionately affected. Given that the trend has been for investors' love for these companies to push their valuations to ever-greater highs – and given that all trends eventually reverse – this is a major risk factor for an investor who just wants a nice smooth ride.

That's why informed investors – those who've done more than watch a few YouTube videos and have taken the time to sit down with a financial professional or read a book or two – will probably have taken their quest for diversification a step further.

THE NAME'S BOND

Whenever the stock market is rocky, bonds become more appealing. Between 2013 and 2023, more than $100 trillion of extra debt was issued globally – all willingly snapped up by institutions and individuals. And for good reason.

Rather than owning a piece of the upside when things go well, as you do with shares, when you buy a bond you're *lending* money. Imagine your friend is starting a business and comes to you for funding: if you lend her £1,000 to be paid back in a year's time that's like a bond, whereas if you gave her £1,000 in exchange for 5 per cent of all her future profits you're effectively buying shares.

As well as lending to companies, you can lend to national governments and, in some countries, to local or regional governments. When a company or a government issues a bond, they're committing themselves to pay you a fixed return: they'll pay you a certain amount of interest each year, then give your money back in full on an agreed future date. Bonds are issued for a term of anything from a few months to multiple decades. Apple, for example, issued corporate bonds with a thirty-year term in 2020, and thirty years is also the current maximum duration of US and UK government bonds.

Much like stocks, most people don't hold individual bonds. It's more common to buy into bond funds, which in turn contain hundreds or thousands of bonds – buying and selling them with the aim of maximising return or replicating the performance of an index. This is what allows the value of bonds to rise and fall: while your return on an individual bond would be completely predictable if you held it all the way through until it was repaid, at different times the market will be willing to pay very different prices to buy that bond 'second hand', based on a whole range of different factors.

Although the value of bonds in the market can change, the relative certainty of the cashflows they produce makes bonds inherently less risky than stocks: however bad things get, the issuer must make payments or face major repercussions. When you're lending to the government of a major country that controls its own currency, the risk is as low as it gets. A loan to the US government for up to one year is even considered in financial circles to be 'risk free', and the rate of interest it pays serves as the benchmark against which all other returns are measured.

With less risk comes less reward. In the US, in a pattern which is representative of most major economies, the long-term return on bonds has been around 6 per cent per year – compared with 10 per cent for the stock market. But while returns have been lower, the ride has been smoother: bonds are less volatile than stocks, meaning that their value bounces around less from year to year. Mixing in some bonds with your stocks, then, should blunt the ups and downs of your portfolio.

This diversification benefit is enhanced by the fact that you'd generally expect the stock market and the bond market to perform well at different times. When all is good in the world and people are feeling positive, investors want a piece of the upside – so will be willing to pay more for companies' shares, believing they'll go up further. When there's more nervousness, owning bonds is more appealing because companies and governments have no choice but make the agreed interest payments. So, in troubled times, investors will demand more bonds and therefore push up their price. In investment lingo, you'd say that stocks and bonds are negatively correlated: when one goes up, the other goes down.

The advantages of bonds have been common knowledge for a long time. In his 1949 book *The Intelligent Investor*, Benjamin Graham wrote: 'as a fundamental guiding rule . . . the investor should never have less than 25 per cent or more than 75 per cent of his funds in common stocks, with a consequent inverse range of between 75 per cent and 25 per cent in bonds.' A large part of Harry Markowitz's legacy with Modern Portfolio Theory was mathematically formalising this rule of thumb, allowing the 'correct' amount of bonds to be built into investors' portfolios based on their desired level of risk and return.

These twin benefits of bonds – lower volatility, and an inverse relationship with stocks – were in full effect during the first two decades of the twenty-first century. Their finest moment came during the 2007–2008 financial crisis, when bond markets soared and helped to offset plunges in stock markets worldwide. This success drew trillions of dollars of wealth into stock/bond portfolios, and anyone lucky enough to have hit their peak investing years during this time saw their wealth compound dramatically.

THE 'SAFE INVESTMENT' THAT WASN'T

Then came 2020. In response to the Covid pandemic, governments around the world responded with unprecedented levels of stimulus – cutting interest rates from already low levels, injecting new money into the system, and stimulating economic activity. In the process, their actions inverted the prevailing relationship between stocks and bonds. All of a sudden they were moving in the same direction.

As it happened, that direction was 'upwards' – so no one was complaining. Yet in 2022 came a dramatic reversal. The stock market had one of its worst years ever. And, to general astonishment, the bond market simultaneously had its absolute worst year of all time.

This period was remarkable for two reasons. First, those 'less volatile' bonds suddenly became a whole lot more volatile. According to market data service Morningstar, bond volatility more than doubled in the years 2022 and 2023 compared to the preceding seven years. Their volatility remained lower than that of the stock market, but still: the calming effect of bonds was blunted. Second, they started moving in the same direction as the stock market – first rising in tandem, then sharply falling. In fact, 2022 was the first time in history that the US stock and bond markets had both fallen by double-digit percentages: a very positive, and very painful, correlation. Having been sitting at a correlation level of -0.6 pre-pandemic (only fractionally off an all-time low), they soared to a positive level of 0.6. The result? With the bond market having such a cataclysmic year – making the plunging stock market look peachy by comparison – those 'cautious' 60/40 investors ended up suffering more than the risk-takers who stuck to stocks.

This wasn't the first time stocks and bonds had moved in the same direction: this was also the standard pattern from the early 1970s through to the late 1990s. What caused the correlation to flip again in the 2020s?

As it happens, the blame for both increased bond volatility and a positive stock/bond correlation lies with the same variable: inflation. Inflation – or more accurately, heightened inflation expectations – is equally bad news for both types of investment. At times when inflation is a concern, bond returns suddenly look less attractive. Investors start to worry that the fixed income they offer will be eroded by inflation, so aren't willing to pay such high prices to acquire them. Stocks can also perform badly under these conditions: companies suffer from the cost of raw materials increasing, and they're less able to finance growth by borrowing money. As a result, stocks and bonds both move in the same direction – and it's a bad one.

If inflation fades from people's minds and goes back to seeming like a problem from another era – as it did for the first two decades of the twenty-first century – the combination of stocks and bonds will probably start offering the same degree of protection that it did before. But as I argued in Chapter 1, it seems likely that we're in for an era of inflation that's both higher and more volatile than we've become used to. Just as it seems to be under control, it will spike up again – meaning it will never be far from people's minds.

If this turns out to be the case, stocks and bonds will both suffer from these flare-ups in tandem – meaning that owning both will do less to protect you than it has done in the past.

IS TRUE DIVERSIFICATION A REALISTIC AIM?

Clearly, achieving a nicely diversified Maintain bucket won't be easy. You could argue that it's unnecessary too: given that shares have historically achieved higher returns, investors who want to grow their wealth as much as possible over the long term would be rational to just put 100 per cent of their Maintain bucket into the stock market and ride out the dips. Indeed, they should even welcome any dips as opportune moments to buy more.

There are problems with this, though. One is that not all

investors are taking such a long-term view: for someone approaching the stage where they plan to live off the proceeds of their Maintain bucket, a sudden dive in value can be actively disastrous rather than merely scary. For this reason, people tend to dial down the risk in their portfolio over time by increasing the proportion of bonds they hold. But if correlations are positive and bonds are more volatile, they'll need to dial down the risk even further to end up in the same place. This reduction in risk would be expected to reduce the size of their returns too.

And there's a psychological problem that affects everyone, regardless of their stage on the investing journey: giant drops in your wealth aren't pleasant, and many people don't have the stomach for them. I do know a handful of people who, when the stock market dropped sharply in 2020 and again in 2022, took the completely rational view that the market was 'on sale' – and piled everything they had into buying more. But these hardy few were far, far outnumbered by the people I know who pulled out of the market for good. This took a potential disaster and turned it into an actual disaster: by selling, they both locked in the loss and gave up any possibility of future gains.

Sure, if you have twenty-plus years ahead of you and you can prove to yourself that you have the iron stomach to hold firm whatever the market throws at you (maybe you were one of those brave few running towards the burning building in 2020), then forgoing diversification could work. If you're investing with the very long term in mind, a Maintain bucket made up of 100 per cent stocks isn't crazy. If history is any kind of guide, you'll most likely be rewarded for your courage in the end.

But for most of us, giving up on diversification altogether isn't realistic. That means that, faced with inherent and growing uncertainty, we're left with one bad option – and one good one. The bad option is, unfortunately, where most investors are today: suffering from fake diversification. They believe they've done the sensible thing and dampened down their returns in exchange for more certainty, only to be at risk of getting hit just as hard as their more aggressive counterparts when things go bad. This, it seems to me, may be a likely outcome for anyone who has adopted the traditional approach of counterbalancing their stock market investments with bonds alone.

The good option is to venture beyond the world of stocks and bonds, and continue the quest for true diversification by bringing other assets into the mix. Sure, it may still involve sacrificing performance compared to stocks alone – but it also allows for the potential of building a Maintain bucket that you can confidently keep topping up during an era when inflation will never be far from our minds.

THE QUEST FOR ALL-WEATHER PERFORMANCE

Harry Browne was a politician who hated politicians. The US presidential candidate for the Libertarian Party in 1996 and 2000, his platform was based on starving the state: removing the federal government from health care and education, ending the War on Drugs, and embracing a foreign policy that 'wishes good will toward people everywhere and is a threat to no other country'. Perhaps surprisingly for a campaign that also promised to abolish income tax, he never secured more than 0.4 per cent of the popular vote.

But his influence in the field of investment has been more enduring. Given his general distrust of government, Browne was dubious about the ability of centralised institutions to keep economic storms at bay – and wanted to help individuals to safeguard their investments, regardless of what the world threw at them. In his 1981 book *Inflation-Proofing Your Investments*, he introduced the concept of the 'Permanent Portfolio': one designed to thrive across four potential future financial regimes that he'd identified.

He observed that stocks produce a strong return in times of prosperity, and bonds guard against deflationary busts. But economies also go through both periods of inflation and protracted recessions, and during these conditions the typical stocks/bonds portfolio has little protection to offer.

The Permanent Portfolio was designed to be made up of just four assets, each given a 25 per cent allocation. Stocks and bonds both feature, and alongside them he added gold to offer protection during periods of inflation and cash as a safety measure for recessions. For a passive investor, this is about as simple as it gets: Browne recommended adjusting once per year to bring the allocations back to 25 per cent each if they'd drifted out of alignment, and otherwise doing nothing whatsoever. There's no need to anticipate what might be around the corner, because the Permanent Portfolio is set up to survive regardless.

If you review its performance since 1972, you've got to hand it to Harry: if 'no surprises' is the goal, his portfolio has delivered. If you'd favoured a more aggressive option and instead invested purely in stocks (I'm assuming a blend of 50 per cent US stocks and 50 per cent international stocks, to roughly approximate a representative global mix), you would at one point have experienced a peak-to-trough drop of 55 per cent. That is, in anyone's book, nasty: it's all well and good to talk about 'being greedy when others are fearful', but most people aren't mentally equipped to see half of their wealth wiped out. If you'd opted to use the Permanent Portfolio, though? The biggest drop was a still unpleasant but much more survivable 16 per cent.

Of course, there are no free lunches (and if there were, Harry would want the government to cut them). So as you'd expect, his portfolio's performance has been lower too. Despite the absolutely disastrous drop of the 'stocks only' portfolio, if you'd

The Diversification Myth

invested $10,000 into it in 1972 you still would have ended up with $264,000 by 2024. This represents an annual return of just under 9 per cent per year. The Permanent Portfolio only managed 6.4 per cent, which would have taken the same $10,000 to just $106,000. That's a big difference.

Would you want to implement the Permanent Portfolio exactly as it was first conceived? I'd say probably not – primarily because of its heavy weighting to cash. Cash is the true 'when all else fails' asset: everything else can crash, but a dollar bill will always be a dollar bill. However, it also can't rise in value, and it doesn't generate any income. So for the majority of the time, it's weighing your portfolio down.

And, today, there's arguably less need for the security offered by cash. Since the Permanent Portfolio was developed, politics has not moved in the direction that Harry was fighting for: governments are involved in an ever-increasing proportion of our lives, and their activity accounts for a greater proportion of overall spending than ever before. As a result, their debts have ballooned and they've allowed the debts of the private sector to do the same, meaning the system just can't handle much in the way of recession. As we saw in 2007–2008 with the financial crisis, again in 2020 with Covid, and in many smaller ways at other times, a growing economy is the only acceptable type of economy: whenever that's under threat, central banks swing into action and do whatever it takes to return to growth.

This means that recessionary periods may be shorter than in the past, rendering the protective benefits of cash effective during narrower windows of time. Of course, you still want to hold cash in your Protect bucket, but having it also make up a quarter of your Maintain bucket seems like a stretch.

Nevertheless, the Permanent Portfolio nicely illustrates the potential benefits of diversifying beyond stocks and bonds. If we forget about Browne's exact picks and percentages but stay true to the general principle that broader diversification is better in a world where stocks and bonds are less complementary than they have been in the past, what could we consider adding into the mix to achieve an adequately diversified portfolio that's built for the twenty-first century?

Gold

Harry Browne included gold in the Permanent Portfolio because its limited supply means it should perform well under inflationary conditions.

Gold has been around for thousands of years and is seen as a 'safe haven' asset: when investors become worried about the health of government-issued currencies and the financial system as a whole, they flee to gold. Unlike currencies, which can be printed at will, there's only so much gold you can pull out of the ground: it tends to be enough to increase the total supply by around 2 per cent per year, and there's not much you can do to speed it up. As a result, over the extremely long term it's proven to be an incredible inflation hedge – meaning that an ounce of gold would buy you the same quantity of 'real world' assets today as it would have done in the distant past. Believe it or not, a house would have cost the same amount of gold in 1979 as it did in 2024, despite obviously costing many multiples more in dollars, pounds or euros. It's even estimated that a men's suit costs the same amount of gold today as a toga would have done in ancient Rome.

This is fantastic if you're planning on investing for thousands of years, but over shorter periods its record is less consistent: in the 1970s it would have protected investors from the rampant inflation of the day, but it did very little to offer any protection during the inflationary period of 2020–2022. Nevertheless, if inflation is a worry (and it surely is), gold is likely to be worth

The Diversification Myth

having. If you took a 60/40 stocks/bonds portfolio and whipped 10 per cent off each to allocate to gold instead, over the past fifty years this would have blunted the worst of the drops without detracting from performance too much. If the future is more inflationary than the recent past, it could do even better.

Bitcoin

Then there's another asset that no investors held in the 1970s, or even during the 2008 financial crash – because it didn't exist. Bitcoin has been called 'digital gold' because it has the same scarcity characteristics as the shiny metal: there's a hard cap of 21 million coins that will ever be issued, so in theory investors (if they believe in its value) should flock to it during times of unrest. In practice, it's behaved more like the most hyped of stocks – flying up in value when markets are flush with cash, then crashing hard.

This caught the attention of fund manager Charlie Morris. Why, he wondered, were these two 'hard currency' assets performing so differently – and did this, in fact, create an opportunity? Morris noticed that – like stocks and bonds are supposed to – gold and Bitcoin have consistently demonstrated a low natural correlation. By holding the two in the right proportions, an investor benefits from Bitcoin boosting gold's returns during good times, while gold calms Bitcoin's crashes during bad times.

Morris's BOLD index (calculated by rebalancing a portfolio of Bitcoin and gold each month) has, since 2015, dramatically out-performed even the best-performing stock markets (the S&P 500 and Nasdaq), with surprisingly low volatility.

Property

Browne didn't include property in the Permanent Portfolio, but once you look beyond stocks and bonds it's the next most common investment choice in much of the world. I'm not talking about your own home here: you'll remember that I've consigned that, despite your grumbles, to the Protect bucket. But as a pure investment there are thought to be 2.3 million holders of buy-to-let property in the UK, and there are an estimated 19.3 million rental homes in the US.

A benefit of real estate compared to cash is that it generates an income, so regardless of economic conditions it's contributing to your overall performance by generating a rental profit. Unlike cash, stocks or bonds, it's highly illiquid: it takes months to sell even when the property market is booming. This is a drawback, yet in a funny way is also a big part of the reason people tend to succeed with it: panic-selling isn't an option. If buy-and-hold for the long run is the right thing to do (and it generally is), property is an investment that protects you from your worst impulses.

Another benefit of property is that it tends to perform well under inflationary conditions: even during the high inflation of the 1970s, real estate managed to keep pace while both stocks and bonds struggled.

Even over the much longer term, it tends to keep pace with inflation because there's always a constraint on its supply: the hard limit on buildable land, the amount of materials and labour needed to build it, and constraints around desirable locations mean that even when the economy is in full swing and enthusiasm is off the charts, there's only so much that can be built.

So, could property be a helpful addition to our Maintain bucket? We can approximate its effects by taking the cash out of Harry Browne's Permanent Portfolio and adding Real Estate Investment Trusts (or REITs) in its place. The data here only goes back to 1994, but since then this particular allocation would have achieved an annual return of 7.44 per cent. This is better than a 60/40 stocks/bonds portfolio performed – and, in a rare cake-and-eating scenario, had a lower maximum peak-to-trough drop and no more volatility. History won't necessarily repeat and I'm not saying 'forget cash and buy property instead', but it's one example of how it is theoretically possible to diversify beyond stocks and bonds while limiting the amount of upside you give up.

Just bear in mind that if you buy an investment property using a mortgage – rather than buying it outright in cash, or holding it indirectly via a fund – the extra risk (and potentially extra return) will shift it into your Improve bucket. We'll see why in the next chapter.

HOW TO BUILD A FUTURE-PROOF MAINTAIN BUCKET

Where does this leave us in our quest for true diversification? A little confused, probably. Once you broaden out from stocks and bonds, the number of options soon becomes overwhelming. And we've only covered the big ones: for the benefit of our collective sanity, I haven't gone near commodities, TIPS, private equity, or any number of other asset classes that are often added into the mix.

Even with the small number of assets we've covered, it's easy to drive yourself mad trying to work out what you should own, and in which proportions. In reality, it's impossible to know what the right decision is: you can only guess about what the financial world might be like in the future, and further guess how each asset might perform in those conditions based on what's happened in the past.

In a way, I find this reassuring. It's clear that owning a bit of everything helps – but as there's no definitive 'right answer' lurking out there if you look hard enough, it's not worth stressing about the details too much. In fact, in playing around with historical data since the year 2000, I've struggled to produce more than a 1 per cent difference in average annual performance even when making substantial changes to my model portfolio. That's not insignificant over a long timeframe, but nor is it the difference between riches and ruin.

You need to have some kind of basis on which to make a decision, so my approach is to start by working out how much of your Maintain bucket you want in stocks. This has historically represented the growth engine of a portfolio, so the answer might be 100 per cent if you have a multi-decade timeframe and an appetite for risk. If it is: well, that was easy. If not, then make your best estimate of how far to dial back your allocation to stocks. You can use typical model portfolios as a guide – such as 60 per cent in the classic 60/40 portfolio, or as little as 25 per cent in the Permanent Portfolio.

Then just fill in the gaps with whatever you're most drawn to, with 'a bit of everything' being a perfectly reasonable answer. The past may not be a reliable guide to the future, but you can test out how different allocations would have performed historically using an online tool if you want to, such as portfoliovisualizer.com. Whatever you decide on, use index funds or cheap Exchange Traded Funds (ETFs) to buy into your chosen assets, because the one thing we know for sure is that the high fees of actively managed funds will always take a chunk out of your returns, whatever the economic conditions.

Once you've done that, remember the compounding principles from the last chapter: you've diversified, so now you need to automate your investments and stay consistent so the end result is effortless. Most importantly of all, *don't keep checking* – because whenever you do, you'll see that some of your investments are doing badly. That's an inevitable consequence of diversification, but seeing that you've lost money can still mess with your mind.

The Diversification Myth

In fact, all you need to do is check in once per year to rebalance. For example, to keep things simple, let's imagine you decided on a 50/50 mix of stocks and bonds. If stocks had a good year and grew in value while bonds had a bad year and fell in value, you might find that your mix has drifted to 55/45. Given that you chose 50/50 for a reason, you need to bring it back into balance – in this case, by selling some stocks and buying some bonds. This involves, counterintuitively, selling what's done well and buying what's done poorly. You'll naturally be reluctant to do this, but it's the only way of avoiding a portfolio that becomes ever more biased to whatever has performed best in the past and is therefore more at risk of a nasty crash.

Above all, I find it helpful to zoom out from all this perplexing detail and remember Ashvin Chhabra's core insight: this is all just one bucket, and whatever you put within it, it's all designed to do the same job. If you're relying on it to protect you, you'll be frustrated: there will be occasional double-digit drops, whatever you do. If you're hoping it will dramatically change your lifestyle within the next couple of decades, disappointment lurks again. However you crack it, you're most likely to make an average annual return of somewhere from 5 to 9 per cent per year. Eventually that adds up to something wonderful, but if you're enviously eyeing the latest Mercedes S-Class or fancy having your name on the side of a museum one day, you'll be needing to bust one final myth.

7

MYTH Ventures like stock-picking and starting a business are insanely risky. Most people should stay well away.

REALITY If you want financial freedom without waiting for decades, you'll need to take some risks – and the trick is to work out which ones are right for you.

CHAPTER 7

THE 'TOO RISKY' MYTH

YouTuber James Dumoulin spent years travelling around the United States asking the same, blunt question: 'How did you get rich?' From Dallas to Las Vegas to Miami, he approached people boarding yachts and parking supercars, hanging out on the golf course or emerging from luxury stores.

Their answers were wide-ranging, with common themes including investing in real estate, starting a business and working in finance. But one response was conspicuous by its absence: 'I bought a diversified collection of index funds and waited.'

On the face of it, this seems to contradict the bulk of mainstream financial advice. After all, haven't we all been told that the route to wealth is through diversifying and waiting, and that it's a mug's game to attempt otherwise? In the words of the classic personal finance book by Thomas J. Stanley, *The Millionaire Next Door* (1996): 'Wealthy individuals are often conservative in their investment approach. They avoid speculative, high-risk investments and focus on preserving their capital through diversification.' Or consider *The Bogleheads' Guide to Investing* (2009) by Mel Lindauer, Michael LeBoeuf and Taylor Larimore: 'Diversification spreads risk and helps protect your portfolio from significant losses. Avoid leverage, as it can amplify losses and lead to financial ruin.' Why do these books, like virtually all mainstream financial advice, warn us away from making big bets, borrowing money and taking risks, when this appears to be exactly how people in the real world actually become rich?

The answer to this apparent contradiction comes down to how wealthy you want to be, and when. It is, in a limited way, true that it's foolish to try to beat the market. In the context of your Maintain bucket, 'diversify and wait' is absolutely the right thing to do: any effort you put into out-performing the average will suck up lots of your time and focus for a minimal improvement at best, and may even result in you doing worse. Most people should – and do – put most of their assets into the Protect and Maintain buckets and make peace with the idea of putting their fate in the hands of the markets.

But as we've seen, this ignores the third motivation: the desire to significantly improve your quality of life from where it is now, rather than just to maintain your current level throughout life. And that's where our Improve bucket comes in.

HOW RICH DO YOU WANT TO BE?

Obviously, there are plenty of older people who live comfortably if unflashily thanks to a lifetime of earning well, living within their means and investing sensibly. But there are no young supercar drivers who fit that profile. So the deceptively simple question to ask yourself is: what do you really want?

Because if you do want to significantly upgrade your lifestyle, you need to acknowledge this motivation and recognise that it involves a separate bucket of assets with totally different characteristics. For the most part, people don't make this mental separation. This results in them taking bigger risks than they should in their Maintain bucket, or owning a rag-tag bunch of investments that are neither safe enough to guarantee long-term security nor ambitious enough to make a meaningful difference.

Not everyone does aspire to such an upgrade. If you have no appetite for risk, or you're perfectly happy with your lifestyle as it is now (you'd just like to maintain it with less work), there's no need for an Improve bucket at all. The upside won't be worth it – and any attempt to make this type of investment comes with two significant drawbacks.

The first is that it's the only bucket where risks can't be offset through diversification, and losses may be permanent. While you can have certainty that your Protect assets will do their job and a high degree of confidence that your Maintain assets will do the same if you give them long enough, you can only attempt to reach your aspirational goals through your Improve assets. And if it goes wrong, that attempt can send you further backwards than forwards. All in all, the range of outcomes is far bigger: you could win big, but you could lose big too.

The second is that it's also the only bucket that involves an investment of time and effort as well as money. None of the investments that fit into the Improve bucket are of the 'set and forget' variety, and nor can you start out in these investments by doing a minimal amount of research and clicking a few buttons. Most people have plenty of things they'd rather do than decide which shares to buy, analyse property deals or research investments in private companies. Yet if you want outsized returns, activities like these are unavoidable.

Clearly, the prospect of success needs to be exciting enough for you to bother taking the risk and putting in the time – and maybe, for you, it's not. But as it becomes harder for the average person to even achieve 'comfortable' status – wage growth has stagnated, inflation has bitten, and the falling interest rates that have benefited all investments have reversed – more and more people are being drawn (or driven) to taking aspirational risks.

Indeed, the less appealing the average becomes, the more risk-taking behaviour we see. Investing in 'penny stocks' (risky bets on small, volatile companies) more than tripled in the five years to 2024 and now makes up 14 per cent of all US trading volume. Sports betting and Forex trading are advertised everywhere.

Altcoins and NFTs have gone to the moon and back again. 'Finance influencers' on social media have attracted millions of followers by shouting about how you can get rich with dropshipping or affiliate marketing. Everyone seems to be trying (or selling) something that promises to offer a way out. And those who aren't actively trying something are engaged in wishful thinking instead: Google searches for 'manifesting' have more than doubled since 2020.

But it's not the desire that's the problem: it's the method. To pursue your aspirational goals safely, there are two things you need to do. The first is not to risk everything, which you accomplish by sizing your Improve bucket appropriately. We covered this back in Chapter 3, and will return to it in the Conclusion too. The second is to take the right kind of risks – and pursue investments that are proven to lead to success rather than to gamble or get sucked in by a get-rich-quick scheme.

As long as you do those two things, you can safely ignore (in your Improve bucket only) all the sober and sensible investment advice you see about diversification, risk minimisation and avoiding debt. Because, as it happens, doing the reverse is a pretty neat summary of how you do get rich.

TO BE COMFORTABLE, DIVERSIFY; TO GET RICH, FOCUS

As Ashvin Chhabra noted when reflecting on the wealthy clients he came into contact with, 'The super-rich did not earn their wealth by building conventional portfolios based on the principles of asset allocation and diversification. In fact, they did just the opposite.' He identified three top-level features of the type of investments and behaviours that led to outsized results: leverage, concentration and human capital.

In the rest of this chapter, we'll take a tour through each. But

The 'Too Risky' Myth

unlike the Maintain bucket, where the conclusion was 'do a bit of all of these', in the Improve bucket you'll most likely need to restrict yourself to just one. In fact, any attempts at diversification will *increase* the level of risk. Each of these investments requires time and skill – and what are the chances that you'll have the capacity and ability to successfully invest in property, pick winning shares *and* run a business? You're more likely to spread yourself too thin, and end up making mistakes that lose you money.

If you look at the most successful investors in the world, they're not generalists: despite having all day every day to dedicate to nothing but the craft of investing, they choose to restrict themselves to mastering a particular asset class or style of investment. Take 'The Bond King', Bill Gross, whose moniker rather gives away his specialism. By mastering bond trading, he built up his company, PIMCO, into one of the biggest funds in the world, managing more than $2 trillion in assets. Then there's Barry Silbert, who used his technical knowledge of the US bankruptcy code to become a billionaire several times over. And the Candy brothers, Christian and Nick, who've built up an estimated £1.5 billion net worth from luxury property development, certainly didn't 'diversify' by dabbling with a bit of stock-picking on the side while building their empire.

'Focus' is one of the most terrifying words in the English language, because it forces you to make an uncomfortable choice: if you commit to one particular type of investment, you're by definition saying 'no' to all the others. But it's unavoidable, and ultimately you should be guided by what you feel the most drawn to. Whatever you choose, you're going to be spending a heck of a lot of time on it – so it had better be something you enjoy.

My aim in this chapter isn't to put you in a position where you know enough that you can get started with any of these areas: that would be impossible. Instead, I'll explain why each is a potential candidate for your Improve bucket and what the main risks and rewards tend to be. From there, it's over to your own research – and if you have no desire to do that research, you might want to return to Chapter 2 and see if you can achieve the same lifestyle improvement by beefing up your earnings instead.

LEVERAGE: GET RICH WITH SOMEONE ELSE'S MONEY

Most of us, if we have a relationship with debt at all, would rather not. Your own mortgage is something you want to be rid of as soon as possible. Credit card debts are to be avoided at all costs. Student loans follow you around acting as a drain on your finances for years.

I grew up in the early 1990s – a time when property prices in the UK had recently crashed and interest rates had spiked – and all I seemed to hear the grown-ups around me talking about was how stressed they were about their mortgages. I barely understood what they were talking about but I could pick up on the panic. I remember thinking to myself, 'one way or another, I'll make sure I never have one of those'. Well, don't ask me for next week's lottery numbers, because my predictive powers are clearly a bit off: I now have quite the collection of mortgages, and I have them to thank for a substantial proportion of my wealth.

This is because, thankfully, I later learned that it's possible to use debt as a tool. When applied to a financial investment, debt is typically referred to as *leverage*. This is an apt term because just as with a lever, it applies a magnifying force – positive or negative – to your investment returns. This is, quite simply, because the debt is allowing you to make bigger investments than you'd be able to with your own money alone.

It's possible to apply debt as a magnifying force to a portfolio

The 'Too Risky' Myth

of shares but in practice few people do: the characteristic volatility of shares means your debt can quickly become too high as a proportion of your assets and get you into trouble. That's why it's far more common to use leverage when making real estate investments – where the sheer difficulty of buying, selling and even knowing quite what your property is worth on any given day masks its volatility and makes it the perfect asset to attach a loan to.

Let's say you borrow 75 per cent of a property's purchase price, and put in the rest using your own cash. This means for every £1 you're putting in, the bank is putting in £3 – or to look at it another way, if you can afford to pay £100,000 in cash for one property, you could use a mortgage to buy four properties for £100,000 each instead. Naturally there's a cost for borrowing this money, which is your interest payment.

The reward (and the risk) come in when you consider the effect this has on your gains (and losses) when house prices change. Imagine you bought a single £100,000 property with all your own cash, and after a year its value had gone up by 5 per cent. What gain did you make? No prizes for working out it's £5,000, or 5 per cent.

But what if you bought four properties for £100,000 each, by putting £25,000 of your own cash into each and taking out four £75,000 mortgages. When each of those homes goes up in value by 5 per cent, that's a total gain of £20,000 – which represents 20 per cent of the money you put in. The use of leverage has multiplied your returns by four.

In practice, there are costs in buying a property that you can't borrow against – such as taxes and legal fees – and so the numbers work out slightly differently for every purchase by the time you've factored this in. But my personal shortcut is to assume that by borrowing 75 per cent of the purchase price – a level often considered to be a safe maximum by residential property investors – you can multiply your returns by three rather than four.

This is what gives leveraged property investment its potential to make big returns. Even if the value of your property only goes up by 2 per cent per year on average from the time you buy it – which is only in line with what inflation is targeted to be – multiply by three and your investment is growing by 6 per cent before you've counted a penny in rent. Given that property growth in the US and UK has historically outpaced inflation, and the inflation figure itself has averaged more than the 2 per cent target since it was first adopted, those could be considered conservative assumptions. If you believe 4 per cent annual growth is plausible, that gives you a 12 per cent annual return – again, before even thinking about the rental income.

As these examples show, it's not that property is anything that special as an asset: it's the ability to use leverage that brings most of the benefits.

Of course, leverage introduces risk and it cuts both ways. If the figures in my examples had gone the other way, you'd need to multiply the loss by three as well. However, as with gains, this only becomes a real (rather than paper) loss if you sell the property for less than you paid for it and lock the loss in. Even if you were unlucky enough to buy the day before a property crash and see 20 per cent instantly wiped off its value (that's 60 per cent of your investment once you've multiplied by three), you can be close to certain that it'll recover its value eventually – and, in the meantime, the rental profit means you'll be paid to wait.

I've already declared my bias here, but naturally there are downsides too. The most obvious of these is the risk around your borrowing costs. When you first take out a mortgage, you'll need to make sure that the rental income comfortably covers your mortgage payments and leaves enough over to account for

The 'Too Risky' Myth

the property's other running costs. However, in many countries (including the UK, Canada and Australia, but excluding the US), it's rare to be able to fix your interest rate for more than five years. What if you borrow at a 4 per cent interest rate then it suddenly spikes to 12 per cent when it's time to renew after five years? Your interest payments have tripled – and you can't just increase the rent to cover the difference, so you might be unable to pay the mortgage without putting in some of your own cash from elsewhere. This puts you at risk of being forced to sell the property – and if you're forced to sell at a time when prices have fallen, then you've locked in the leveraged loss that you were trying to avoid. Luckily, since interest rates have made their abrupt and dramatic return to their historical norms, this risk is lower than it was – finally, an advantage to the ending of the 'free money' era that has caused investors so much trouble.

In common with anything else in the Improve bucket, this is clearly not a hands-off, let-it-compound-over-time endeavour. Unless you want to become one of those viral 'evil landlord' stories doing the rounds on social media, you have a time-consuming responsibility to respond to your tenants' messages about non-flushing toilets and boilers that predictably pack in just as there's a cold snap. After more than fifteen years, I finally have my property portfolio at a point where it's taking up less than an hour of my time per month – even while I'm still growing it – but it's taken a lot of work and mis-steps to get there.

Applying leverage to property allows you (if it goes well) to compound your wealth significantly faster than by making unleveraged investments in your Maintain bucket, meaning it will make a noticeable difference to your lifestyle sooner. You can also turn up the risk dial even further in search of results that are faster still, by undertaking development projects where you can sell for a profit quickly rather than waiting multiple years for prices to rise.

CONCENTRATION: INVEST WHERE YOU HAVE AN EDGE

If you'd bought shares in the payment processing company Square in 2019, you would have paid around $70 for them – and been delighted when you'd virtually tripled your money two years later. Yet if you'd chosen a different payment processor to buy – German company Wirecard, say – you'd have been horrified to watch their share price plunge from £150 to mere pennies in the same timeframe.

This is an extreme yet not particularly uncommon example of the opportunity and risk that comes from taking concentrated positions. In a diversified Maintain bucket made up of index funds, you may have had some exposure to both Square and Wirecard. But given that thousands of other companies would have been in the mix too, even their dramatic differences in fortunes would barely have caused a tremor to register on your investment needle. In contrast, by picking just one of these companies to hold in your Improve bucket, the result could have been life-changing – or resulted in total wipeout.

Were the people pushing shares in GameStop or dog-related cryptocurrencies to ridiculous heights in 2021 'taking a concentrated position'? No, they were taking a punt. The difference between gambling and investing is having some kind of edge: an informational advantage that most people in the market don't have.

I sometimes exploit my informational advantage from being in the property industry by taking both long- and short-term positions. For example, I often have a sense of whether a house-building company's next quarterly results will be impressive or disappointing through interacting with them via my business. In case any lawyers are reading, let's be very clear that this isn't insider trading: I never know anything that someone else couldn't

The 'Too Risky' Myth

find out if they put in the legwork. But mostly, they don't. This allows me to benefit from the bounce in their share price once the results are revealed, then sell to lock in my profit. As another example, I held shares in a particular property fund for years because I believed the market had got the wrong idea about it: people were selling its shares on the basis of a problem that some funds in the sector had, but I knew from experience that this one didn't. It took a long time but eventually my patience paid off: worries about the phantom problem went away, its share price rocketed, and I recently sold for a profit.

This 'edge' can come from exploiting an area of specialist knowledge you already have, or through developing one. This is what makes the Improve bucket so personal: if you've gladly read about the biotech sector for fun, that's great news – because it's likely to be one that expands significantly (lifting all boats) in the coming years. But if the mere thought of reading the results of a drug trial bores you to tears, it's best to stay away.

And that's not all: as well as having all the relevant information, you need to have the psychological traits to capitalise on it. Investing is mentally tough in a way you'd never expect it to be before you start: losing money is scary, even when it's only temporary and only on paper, and it makes even the coolest-headed people do ill-advised things. When the price is dropping you need to somehow work out whether you were wrong and cut your losses, or whether the market is just taking time to realise you were right. And when things are going well, you need to know when it's time to bank your gains and get out – which is arguably even harder.

I'm presenting this as if it's one all-or-nothing bet, but that's not quite the case: you can take some advantage of diversification by taking positions in multiple companies. The limiting factor is your capacity to dig deep and identify genuine opportunities. Strange as it may sound, it could be less risky to invest in two or three companies that you understand deeply than ten companies that you've barely scratched the surface of.

HUMAN CAPITAL: THE ULTIMATE WEALTH CREATION VEHICLE

Many of the millionaires who get accosted on the street by nosey YouTubers have gained their wealth by taking the principle of concentration to another level. They put everything they have into one business: their own.

I know – saying 'to get rich, just start a business' isn't the most immediately actionable financial wisdom you'll ever read. But it's also impossible to ignore: short of being born into it, it's the most common route via which people become wealthy. Its power comes from the fact that it combines all three drivers of Improve-style investments: a concentrated bet, using leverage (either financial, or operational in terms of having employees), which involves a hefty investment of the owner's time, effort and skill.

James Dumoulin's YouTube interviews hint at the wild array of different paths this can take. One person he spoke to was a dentist who realised that he could make dramatically more money if he took his industry knowledge and moved beyond drilling molars: he bought his surgery (a real estate play), then turned it into a business by employing others to work under his umbrella. Another was an engineer who invented a mobile drinking-water trailer that ended up being used at the Olympics, while yet another was an engineering dropout who started a major e-commerce streetwear brand.

Businesses are, of course, not typically something you can dabble in on the side. Even though your time and skills aren't strictly an investment, I still like to think of them as part of your Protect bucket: you can always use them to cover your living costs if your investments take a hit. So, by absorbing your time and preventing you from holding down a job simultaneously, starting a business is risky in terms of lost protection as well as the more obvious pitfalls. For this and many other reasons, starting a business won't be right for most people – but there are other ways to gain access to the same benefits.

If you have the cash and the conviction but not the skills or the desire to go all-in, you can use your Improve bucket to back someone else's venture. This is what Peter Thiel did when he made probably the most famous private investment of all time – putting $500,000 into Facebook in its early days, which became more than a billion dollars when he sold after the company went public.

Investing in other businesses comes in several different forms. One is private equity, which is where investors buy a mature, profitable business with the aim of making it more valuable and re-selling it a few years later. It is unusual for individuals to get involved in directly, and it's more typical to buy into a private equity fund. Unless this represented a huge chunk of your assets on its own, this would count as part of your Maintain bucket because it diversifies across multiple investments. Another is angel investing, which is a high-risk bet in a very early-stage company that's not making a profit and may currently be no more than an idea. Most of these bets don't work out (you never hear about all Peter Thiel's other investments that ended up worthless), but the odd one that succeeds produces such a high return that it covers all the losers and then some. The smallest angel investment tends to be around £5,000, which means it is possible for an individual to make multiple investments (making the venture less absurdly risky) for the same initial outlay as the deposit needed for an investment property.

The main issue in both cases is one of deal-flow: how many fantastic businesses do you tend to chance upon who are willing to hand you a piece of the company in exchange for your money?

There are 'crowdfunding' platforms that aggregate deals, and they have produced a handful of big winners – including Monzo, Oculus and BrewDog – but, unsurprisingly, the best opportunities always go to insiders rather than being opened up to the public.

Still, if you move in the right circles (or are willing to spend the time working your way into them), backing someone else's business is a viable alternative to starting your own. If you have a colleague who's quitting to do their own thing, becoming a minority shareholder in their business can pay off – especially if you have the expertise to validate the opportunity, judge their ability to execute and provide advice along the way.

Even by the standards of the Improve bucket, this type of investment is firmly at the far end of the risk/reward spectrum. Putting everything you have into one opportunity would be madness, which is why it's important to size your Improve bucket correctly to start with, then introduce some amount of diversification within it.

For example, I've made a grand total of one angel investment, into a friend's tech startup. I know that she's brilliant, and I'm excited to be part of the journey. But I'm fully aware that however highly I rate her and see the opportunity, most businesses fail and I'm more likely to lose that money completely than I am to strike it rich. If that investment represented a significant chunk of my investable assets, the risk level would be off the charts. But thankfully for my cortisol levels, it's only a small part of an Improve bucket that also includes my own business and leveraged property investments – and my Improve bucket itself sits alongside the long-term safety and protection of the other two.

'IF I CAN DO IT, ANYONE CAN'

There's one uncomfortable truth that we need to acknowledge about those millionaire interviews: the people who start a business that fails, or attempt a real estate development that bankrupts them, never get a microphone shoved in their face as they go about their daily business. This lionising of the winners while ignoring the losers is known as survivorship bias, and it's the reason that most people overestimate their chances of success in business, investment, or any other field with rare but eye-catching outcomes.

The reviews for this book would probably be better if I told you that as long as you just work hard and believe in yourself, you can have anything you dream of – but I can't. You can never be guaranteed to reach your aspirational goals: all you can do is try, and failure will set you back compared to if you'd just stuck to the Protect and Maintain buckets.

This is why finding the right balance between the three is all-important. Often it's not the nature of the investment itself that makes it a wild all-or-nothing swing or simply a cheap lottery ticket: it's the *size* of the investment. So in the Conclusion we'll bring everything we've covered together into an action plan, and look at some real examples from which you can take inspiration.

CONCLUSION Financial freedom is closer than you think.

CONCLUSION
A MYTH-BUSTER'S GUIDE TO FINANCIAL FREEDOM

When I started uncovering the money myths that I've shared in this book, I felt as surprised as a man who, as Douglas Adams once put it, having believed himself to be totally blind for five years, suddenly discovered that he had merely been wearing too large a hat.

I'd long suspected that putting my faith in the markets wouldn't work out as well for me as it had done for my parents' generation – but I hadn't anticipated quite how off the mark mainstream financial advice would be. However much I swore off oat lattes – or even reduced my rental costs – I couldn't save my way to financial independence. Stocks and bonds were nowhere near as safe a bet as I'd been told. And buying my own home, far from being the ultimate life goal, would be an ineffective use of my money given my future plans.

As I made changes to my financial life to reflect the realities I now understood, something strange happened: I started thinking about money a lot less. It's not like I've renounced all earthly possessions, but now I don't need to give money much thought because I have a simple plan that cuts through all the complexity and uncertainty. I don't need to worry about what will happen to the stock market or the policies a political party might adopt, because I have complete conviction that I'm following an approach that works and where the outcome is under my control.

For me, this transformation took place over a decade as I

Conclusion

randomly uncovered fresh pieces of the puzzle in between making plenty of mistakes that set me further back. For you, it doesn't need to take anywhere near that long because you can make those changes in a logical order, guided by some clear models. So, in this final chapter, I'll set out an eight-step plan that you can follow – and describe what making this transformation might look like for people at all different stages of life.

EIGHT STEPS TO A BETTER FINANCIAL FUTURE

1: Make easy cuts to your spending

We now know it's a myth that you can save your way to wealth. But by embracing mindful spending, you can make some cutbacks without sacrificing anything that's important to you.

If you're not able to put any money into savings and investments at the moment, fixing this is critical because it unlocks every other step: you can't make any progress while you're spending everything you earn. Still, it's not necessarily the case that faster is better. Even if it's possible to make more radical cutbacks, I still advocate for living for today while keeping an eye on tomorrow. This slow and steady approach is more sustainable. And as there are some experiences you can only have while you're younger, it makes no sense to spend decades denying yourself.

2: Get your basic protection in place

Most people would consider it essential that they're protected, highly desirable to be able to maintain their lifestyle, and very nice if they can achieve their aspirational goals. Given this order of importance, it makes sense to lock in at least a basic level of protection before doing anything else.

So you need to start filling your Protect bucket first. At the

Conclusion

very least, this will include an emergency fund – and you can revisit Chapter 4 to be reminded of how to calculate its size. You could argue that, if you're saving up cash for another big protection asset, like a home, you could borrow from these savings if needed: having a separate pot for emergencies just means you have even more cash melting away in the face of inflation. Logically that makes sense, but most people like the mental separation of two distinct pots, and would find it difficult to see their home-owning aspirations set back by having to dip into those savings to cover an emergency.

3: Decide about your home

Maybe I persuaded you with my argument in Chapter 4 that your home won't make you fabulously wealthy, but for a variety of practical and emotional reasons it will still form part of many people's plans. If you own a home already and you're on track to pay the mortgage off, you can skip this step; but if you're still working out whether to try to buy, you have three options.

1. **Prioritise buying a home.** All your savings go towards a deposit – and, of course, you save them in a bank account rather than investing them in anything that could fall in value for a protracted period of time.

2. **Prioritise investments.** Start the compounding process as early as possible by contributing to investments in your Maintain bucket. As your earnings increase in future, you can put the extra money towards the deposit for a home.

3. **Mix and match.** You could invest, say, half of your monthly savings so you're getting the compounding machine started, and put the rest towards a deposit.

Conclusion

There's no right answer to this. No one else can tell you what's right for you to do – in fact, even you don't really know what's right for you, because you're making decisions based on expectations about a future that could change unexpectedly. For example, I know people who'd been saving hard for a home then received a job offer abroad, at which point buying a house suddenly stopped being relevant.

But you have to make the decision as best you can – and in my opinion, that should be a practical and emotional choice rather than a financial one. As Chapter 4 covered, there's nothing magical about a home: building up your ownership of assets is critical, but they don't have to be assets that you live in. When you run the numbers fully and take account of opportunity cost, owning a home is seldom a runaway winner: owning other assets (which could even be an investment property) can work just as well. Because so much can change over time, it's impossible to know which will be the better financial investment. So, instead, focus on lifestyle factors like how much you value safety over flexibility.

For most people, some version of the 'mix and match' option will probably be the way forward. For example, if you have an employer who will match any contributions you make into a pension, this is free money and it will likely make sense to take advantage of it up to the upper limit of the match. Beyond that, any additional savings could go towards a deposit.

4: Calculate your 'bucket' sizes

Catalogue any investments you already have, using what you learned from Chapter 3 to divide them up into Protect, Maintain and Improve. By the end, you should have a pie chart (literally, if you've used a spreadsheet, or the ability to sketch a rough one on the back of an envelope if not) showing you how your investments break down between the three 'buckets'. If you don't have

Conclusion

any investments yet, instead think about what you'd like the balance to be so you know where you're heading.

Next, assess how your actual allocation matches up against what it 'should' be considering your current life situation, your goals, and where you fall personally on the 'fear of loss versus desire for gain' spectrum. If you're anything like me, the disconnect might give you a shock: when I went through this exercise myself, I discovered that my investments were far more cautious than I'd suggest for someone of my age, risk appetite and ability to bounce back from a setback.

You might see yourself as a young, dynamic and ambitious type, and be astonished to find that you have no Improve assets at all – which puts you on track for comfort late in life, but is no good if you're nurturing dreams of upgrading your lifestyle or retiring early. Conversely, you might be a naturally cautious person and discover that you're far too Improve-heavy: you've been picking individual stocks and don't own a home, which could be storing up a nasty shock for next time there's a market crash.

It's important to remember that you're doing this exercise based on where you are today not where you hope to be in the future. Your ideal asset allocation will change over time as your priorities shift, your time horizon shrinks and your attitude changes: it's highly unlikely that you'll think of the same mix of assets as 'ideal' in twenty years' time as you do today. This takes the pressure off. You're deciding on your best guess regarding the right next step, which can be held under constant review; you're not making an irreversible decision that will determine your entire investing life.

5: Audit your Maintain bucket

If you have Maintain-style investments already, revisit them in the light of the diversification myth from Chapter 6. How diversified are they really?

Conclusion

If you're like many people, you'll be very stocks-heavy, probably with a bias towards the US or your home country. Now you understand that this isn't truly diversified and there are a whole range of different scenarios in which they won't protect you, assess how you feel about that: how comfortable would you be with a drawdown of 50 per cent? Would you be willing to smooth out that ride in exchange for a small reduction in performance each year?

If you've recognised the need to rebalance, go back to Chapter 6 and consider which assets you want to bring into the mix to add diversification, and to what extent. You don't necessarily need to do this by selling anything you own now: you could just focus on new assets with your future purchases, so you gradually become more diversified over time.

When you're making this decision, remember: the work you've already done to get the split between buckets right is far more important than finding the perfect split within buckets, so I'd encourage you to just get going without becoming hung up on the details. The difference your decisions make will be minimal, and your time and attention is best saved for future steps. Besides, as you probably won't be making gigantic contributions at the start, the stakes are low and there will be plenty of time to make refinements later.

6: Build your 'compounding machine'

Whether you're adding to your existing Maintain investments or starting from scratch, set yourself up to take advantage of the benefits of compounding without giving it more attention than it deserves. You do this by building a 'machine' that's diversified, automated, effortless and consistent.

The ideal solution is to set up an automatic transfer from your bank account to your investment platform of choice each month,

Conclusion

then set up an automatic recurring order to buy the investments you want to accumulate. If you don't do this, it's highly likely that your faulty 'human software' will cause you to mess it up – whether that's by forgetting, or second-guessing whether it's a good idea to put more money in at any given time. Instead, harness your laziness by making good investing practices happen by default, and ensuring that it requires active effort to deviate from them. The few hours (maximum) it will take you to set this up will give you the highest return on investment of any time you ever spend.

7: Work on earning more

It might be that you've got plenty of investable cash to splash around on filling all your investing buckets. It might be that you're a little short but not by much. Or – less happily – you might be absolutely miles away from being able to invest for your future or improve your life today.

If you're in that last group, you'll be in good company: even after taking the first step of consciously trimming their expenses, most people reading this book won't be able to hit their investment goals right away. When you think about it, it'd be weird if they were: you'd be beyond lucky to find you were in great financial shape before you'd devoted any thought to it, in the same way that you wouldn't expect to be in perfect shape before setting foot in a gym or buying a pair of trainers.

So you'd probably prefer to be in a better position than you are, but just being aware of that gap is a bigger step than it seems – because now you can start doing something about it. And when it comes to doing something about it, there's only one factor that's fully within your control: earning more.

Why is that?

Conclusion

- You've already embraced mindful spending, so you can't cut your expenses any further without sacrificing your lifestyle today.

- You know what you need to be protected, and there's no way of reducing that.

- You can't force the average return of a diversified collection of financial assets to be any higher than it is.

- You can (and maybe will) make bets with a bigger upside in the Improve bucket. But this is a whole new skill to learn, and these investments will take time to pay off.

Earning more, though, is something you can start working on today and you might get a win (even if only a small one) by this time next week. Anything extra you earn will give all your investments a lift, by allowing you to buy more of whatever you're currently targeting.

Whether those extra earnings come from finding a way to get a pay rise, striking out on your own or starting something on the side, look back to Chapter 2 for some ideas.

8: Research 'Improve' investments

Two of your buckets are now taken care of: you've sorted out Protect (in the form of an emergency fund, and steps towards a home if that's a priority for you), and started the compounding contributions that will fill your Maintain bucket.

Let's pause for a moment to recognise what a huge achievement that is: you have a plan in place, that plan will be carried out automatically, and it will secure your future without you needing to take the slightest interest in the financial markets.

But what if you want to get there sooner, and turn left when

Conclusion

boarding planes along the way? Then remember our seventh myth: you can beat the market, within the confines of your Improve bucket at least. If these investments perform well (which, as you'll remember, is based on your time and skill), they'll allow you to improve the quality of your life now, or retire earlier, or just choose the most extravagant cruises when you hit the standard pension age.

Maybe you have a little money left over to allocate to the Improve bucket, but nowhere near enough to get started in your chosen asset class, such as investing in property. That's OK: you can start saving up cash in a dedicated account to go towards this type of investment in future, and build your knowledge by reading and learning about the subject in the meantime. It might not feel like it, but this is the best way to start. It's the people who steam in with lots of money and little knowledge who make the expensive mistakes.

HOW TO PUT YOUR PLAN INTO ACTION

Much as I've tried to give you a simple series of actions to work through, most steps involve you using your own judgement rather than applying some generic 'rule'. And that, as I know from being through this process myself, can feel intimidating.

So even though everyone's situation is unique, it can be helpful and comforting to see what decisions others are making. To do that, let's run through examples of how people in different life situations might update their plans to better reflect financial reality.

House-rich, cash-poor

Mick and Sam are both in their early fifties, and their Protect bucket is overflowing: other than their emergency fund, they've

Conclusion

diverted all their savings into paying off their mortgage. They celebrated their fiftieth birthdays by calling up to make the final over-payment, and popped the cork on a bottle of Cava when they received confirmation that their account had been closed and the house was 100 per cent theirs.

This has put them in a super secure position for today, but they have almost nothing in the way of Maintain or Improve assets that will work for them in the future. Well, they do have something: from being enrolled in their workplace pension schemes for around a decade, they have a grand total of £30,000 in stocks and bonds. If they continue at this pace, they'll still only have £60,000 when they reach pension age – which will give them an income of just £2,400 per year in retirement. They will both qualify for a UK state pension, though. In total, they're on track to end up with a combined retirement income of around £25,000.

That isn't so bad, especially as they also have the option to release some more cash by moving to a smaller house or cheaper location now both their kids have left home. But it's not ideal, because they're relying on the state for virtually all of their income – meaning they can't possibly quit their office jobs until they're sixty-six. Ideally, both would have liked to stop working earlier. They have dreams of travelling the world, and want to do it while they're healthy enough to enjoy all the activities they love.

The good news is that, now they've paid off their mortgage, they can increase their investments. They were previously paying £1,000 a month towards their mortgage, so they add this full amount to their Maintain bucket. This means that by the time they're sixty-five they'll have a much healthier £376,000, allowing them to draw at least £15,000 per year and taking their total retirement income to £36,200.

But that still relies on them working all the way up to the age that government support kicks in. By the time they're sixty,

Conclusion

they'll only be able to take £9,240 from their own investments: not enough to stop working.

Mick and Sam are a prime example of a couple for whom the miracle of compound interest isn't so miraculous, but they have two options to compensate. The first is to put their spare £1,000 per month into Improve rather than Maintain investments. Maybe it's stock picking, maybe it's property, maybe it's something else entirely. But if they manage to compound their investments by 15 per cent per year above the rate of inflation (rather than the 5 per cent I've been assuming), by the time they're sixty they'll be generating an incredible £60,000 per year. That would allow them to quit their jobs at least five years earlier than planned, and travel the world in style. A tall order, and a road rife with risk, but an option nonetheless.

The second is to boost their earnings. By developing his existing skills and connections, Mick might be able to go freelance and earn twice as much for the same amount of work. When they're ready to travel, he might be able to work for clients remotely so they can take long extended trips while he works part-time. Or, instead of putting their extra £1,000 per month into investments, Sam could put it towards starting a new business and aim to hand this business off to an employee to run in five years' time.

By refusing to accept the baseline path, they have options – and in ten years' time their finances could look radically different. Yet because of the stage of life they're at, merely relying on compounding isn't going to do the trick: anything they do will require effort and involve risk.

When investing can wait

Afsheen is twenty-six, and works as a social media manager in a major city earning £28,000 per year. She shares an apartment

Conclusion

with a friend, which absorbs a big chunk of her income and leaves her struggling to save any money at all.

Some of her friends are still living with their parents and saving hard to buy a house, but to Afsheen that sounds unbearable. For a start, she loves living in the city centre, and moving back to suburbia with her family would be too much of a sacrifice for her lifestyle today. On top of that, she has no idea where she'll want to be living in five years' time: she might meet someone and want to move in with them, or even try living and working in a totally different part of the world.

One thing Afsheen does have in her favour is a generous company pension scheme: if she contributes 5 per cent of her salary, her employer will match it with another 5 per cent. She's doing this now while barely noticing, because her contributions are deducted from her pay slip before the salary hits her bank account each month. This will do wonders for her Maintain bucket: by the age of sixty-five (with an average return of 5 per cent above inflation), she'll have accumulated £335,000 – of which only £55,000 was put in by her personally. Of course, this assumes – completely unrealistically – that she never receives a single pay rise, so in reality it will be far better.

With that in mind, Afsheen can be far more upbeat about her finances than it first appears. Even if she's saving nothing today (although after going through the mindful spending audit, she should be able to save something), she'll be fine as long as she resists all-out lifestyle inflation and directs some of her future pay rises to investments. She can even – if she wants to – bias her investments towards the riskier Improve bucket because her Maintain bucket is taking care of itself.

If I were talking to Afsheen, I'd suggest that she doesn't worry too much about investments and instead focuses on setting herself up for some chunky future pay rises. By the time she's forty, she could have risen through the ranks to become a Marketing

Conclusion

Director on a six-figure salary. Alternatively, she could set out to loosen the time–money connection by becoming a freelance marketing consultant, potentially earning even more. Either way, she can use some of the ideas in Chapter 2 to make it happen.

Unlike Mick and Sam, Afsheen has time on her side. This means (with help from a generous employer) her Maintain bucket will build nicely even if the returns aren't stellar. She also, sensibly, knows that putting a house into her Protect bucket isn't right for her at the moment. If she backs this up by taking an intentional approach to her career, she should soon start leapfrogging her friends. The result? She can take full advantage of life now – while automatically setting herself up for a lucrative future.

Taking risks to buy freedom

Amara has recently graduated in law, but she'll never see the inside of a courtroom: on the strength of her academic record and some gruelling interviews, she's secured an Investment Analyst position at a major investment bank. She's starting on a chunky £40,000 salary, but this is just the beginning of her enviable earnings: by the time she's thirty she should comfortably be making £150,000 as a base salary, which could potentially be doubled by bonuses in good years.

Amara has seen both sides of where investment banking can take you. She sees senior colleagues in their fifties earning unholy amounts of money yet still completely reliant on a job that requires them to work punishing sixty-hour weeks. With a big house, holiday home by the coast and children in expensive schools, their lifestyle has inflated to match their earnings. She's also, from friends a few years ahead of her, seen what seems like a smarter approach: spend five years living frugally while earning the big bucks, then quit with a giant savings cushion to pursue

Conclusion

something more enjoyable than working in investment banking (which includes, last time I checked, almost everything).

Amara respects her friends who've chosen that second path but it's not right for her. If she's going to spend her twenties working hard, she wants to play hard and enjoy the lifestyle too – not leave work at 10pm and spend an hour commuting out to the suburbs to live with her parents to save money.

So Amara chooses a third, more unusual path by filling her Improve bucket early. First, she ensures her Protect bucket is nicely topped up by saving up to buy a two-bedroom apartment, and renting the spare room to one of her best friends to partially cover her mortgage. Critically, this isn't a lifestyle compromise for her: she'd choose to live with a friend regardless, and she spends most of her time at work anyway. Then she skips Maintain, correctly recognising that she has so much time on her side it won't make much difference even if she doesn't make any Maintain investments until she's thirty. The stock market might seem like a natural choice for her Improve bucket given her profession, but she finds herself more drawn to property and has some knowledge of it from family members who've built up small portfolios.

By the time she's thirty, she's on track to own seven properties, producing a rental profit of £2,100 per month. That's not an astonishing amount of money, but – accustomed to keeping her living costs low – it's enough to buy her freedom. The regular income (along with a healthy emergency fund) could support her while she spends a few years travelling the world, or give her a cushion to spend time out of work retraining or starting a family, or allow her to step into a role that pays less but is more rewarding (which includes, again, anything).

These are options that Amara will only have while she's still young, and are worth infinitely more than a well-stuffed pension pot that won't be available to her for several more decades. She

Conclusion

won't escape the rat race as quickly as some of her frugal peers but she will also have made the most of being young and living in a big city. And even if it doesn't work out as planned and she makes a series of disastrous investments, she can still sell everything at a manageable loss – and be able to start building again before most people have even got started for the first time.

From zero to early retirement in twenty years

Aidan is thirty years old, and feeling a bit hopeless. He has a job doing . . . well, it's not even worth describing because it's so soul-suckingly dull.

He wants to buy a house with his girlfriend soon because they want to start a family without the worry of a capricious landlord kicking them out. He also has no desire to work until anything like normal retirement age: his dad died young, and he badly wants to be in a position to stop work by the time he's fifty so he can spend plenty of time doing what he loves rather than fiddling around with spreadsheets.

So far, Aidan has drifted. He never did amazingly well at school, but he's smart and loves to learn – he just hasn't deliberately developed any skills yet that are valuable outside his current role. Now, though, shocked into action by his thirtieth birthday, he's ready to make some changes.

Aidan could start taking his career more seriously: studying for qualifications, developing skills and strategically job-hopping, and work towards a much bigger salary in a role that's more fulfilling for him. But he doesn't want to wait that long – and by the time he's finished saving for his house, another fifteen years of compounding won't get him anywhere close to where he wants to be at his target retirement age of fifty.

So Aidan takes advantage of the fact that he's sitting at a desk all day (often at home), and no one seems to have noticed that he

Conclusion

only has about three hours per day of actual work to do. He starts reading up on different online business models, and after six months he starts his own online store selling home fitness equipment – sourcing it from another part of the world, and arranging to ship orders directly to customers without him needing to hold any stock or make big upfront commitments. He starts waking up early so he can put in a couple of hours of focused time before starting his job, and manages to sneak in a fair bit during his working day too.

For a year Aidan makes no money at all. But he's learning, and the business is only costing him around £100 per month to run. In his second year, he makes a profit of £10,000. In his third year, he makes more than he earns from his salary. This means he earns enough in total that, by combining savings with his girlfriend, they can buy their own home.

In his fourth year, he quits his job – and with the extra time he can not only increase his profits even further by putting more time into his business, he can also spend plenty of time with his newborn daughter. By either selling his business or putting a team in place so it can be run by other people, Aidan is comfortably on track to have full control of his time well before the age of fifty.

The disorganised millionaire

Ken is in his early forties, and has been running a telecoms company with one of his best friends since he left school. He's considered selling the business but it doesn't seem to make sense while he still enjoys it: he likes travelling to meet clients, and finds it rewarding to help his younger employees to develop their skills.

The business has had some clients for more than a decade, and its long-term contracts mean it's consistently highly profitable.

Conclusion

The business doesn't need to retain much cash, so Ken and his co-founder split the profits between them – and he always ends up with far more than he needs to cover his lifestyle costs. Despite having kids in an expensive school, multiple overseas holidays and not a single budgeting app on his top-of-the-range iPhone, he never struggles for cash.

Ken has solved the earning part of the equation, but his investments are a mess. He dabbles in shares based on tips from friends, has made a couple of small private investments in companies started by acquaintances, and has owned an investment property for years.

Ken's Protect bucket is full (he owns his home and has more than enough cash) but his Maintain bucket is empty. To make matters worse, he hasn't put the time and focus needed into the assets in his overflowing Improve bucket. If he ran the numbers (which he never has done), he'd probably find that they're performing worse than he could achieve with a boring, diversified collection of Maintain assets. He could even be losing overall, and he wouldn't know.

As long as Ken keeps earning vastly more money than he needs, there are no real consequences beyond making someone like me shudder at the lack of organisation and wasted potential. Indeed, when he comes to sell the business he could end up with a lump sum big enough to last him and his family for ever – but without taking a more structured approach, he risks blowing most of it on 'investments' that are more like gambles.

My advice to Ken would be to stop making any more Improve-type investments for now, and get his Maintain bucket in order. You've already seen that this requires no knowledge of the stock market at all, but Ken could always use a financial advisor if he needs the accountability of having someone make sure he invests consistently and sensibly. Even though he's starting late, he's earning enough that he'll be able to plug the gap – and he could choose to sell some of his more liquid Improve investments to fund it more quickly.

Then, if he develops an interest in a particular Improve-type asset, he'll have ample cash left over to start accumulating it – after doing the research and learning he's skipped up until now. And if he has no interest at all? No problem – his business represents an Improve-type investment anyway. With less time dabbling in investments, there's even the opportunity to give his business more focus and increase its value by acquiring competitors or adding new services.

YOU CAN HANDLE THE TRUTH

It's true: getting ahead financially is harder today than it has been for generations. The simple cut-and-paste approach to investing you've been told to adopt could leave you perilously short. And retirement – those golden years where you finally get to enjoy the fruits of all your hard work – was a historical anomaly that's evaporating just as you approach it. Total downer, hey?

Well, no – not in the slightest. Because since uncovering these myths and putting an alternative plan in place, I've never felt more positive – about my money, my career, and my life in general.

I think the reason comes down to this: even if the 'old' way still worked, it involves putting your faith in other people. Everything is great so long as the financial markets don't collapse, your employer decides to keep you around, and a change of government policy doesn't throw your plans into chaos. An enormous body of research shows that feeling reliant on others is actively bad for your health, both mental and physical.

The approach I've outlined takes the power away from shadowy politicians and opaque financial markets and puts it firmly back in your hands. You can take control of your earnings – maximising the benefit of that most powerful lever, and feeling

Conclusion

empowered by being the one calling the shots. You can save smartly, being mindful of your future without feeling guilty about enjoying today. You can invest intelligently – automating the majority that doesn't matter, and giving your all to the few areas where your efforts and skills make an outsized difference. And you can gradually build a working life that's so fun, flexible and lucrative that you never want to retire from it.

Will it be easy? Of course not: nothing worthwhile ever is. But you don't need to finish the process before you see the benefits. In fact, you'll start to feel better as soon as you take your first steps. Because here's the thing: money is an output. It's the result of all the value you've added, habits you've adopted, and decisions you've made. That means it's impossible to improve your financial life without improving yourself more generally. The actions you take to bolster your bank balance will spill over to other areas of your life, improving your relationships, your mental state, and even your physical health.

That sounds like a grandiose claim from a book that merely set out to debunk some money myths. But I know it's true because it's happened to me – and I've seen it happen to plenty of others too.

Money isn't something to feel intimidated by, anxious over, or guilty about. It's a tool that we can harness to live the best life we can, and to help those we care about do the same. Because money touches every part of our lives, making progress will enrich your life far beyond the number in your bank account. And since you're dealing with realities rather than myths, you can get started right now.

NOTES

INTRODUCTION: NEW GAME, NEW RULES

p. 4   'the number of over seventies in the workforce in the UK has increased by 61 per cent over the past ten years': https://www.theguardian.com/society/2023/apr/30/british-workers-work-into-70s-cost-of-living

p. 4   'in the US it's expected to grow by another 96 per cent in the next five years': https://www.nbcmiami.com/news/local/working-to-live-past-75-why-our-elders-are-still-working-and-not-retiring/3315404/

p. 4   'the share of workers aged fifty-five years or older increased from 12 per cent to 20 per cent between 2004 and 2019': https://ec.europa.eu/eurostat/statistics-explained/index.php?title=Ageing_Europe_-_statistics_on_working_and_moving_into_retirement

p. 6   'total level of debt to GDP practically doubled from just over 100 per cent in 1971 to 195 per cent by 2007': https://www.imf.org/en/Blogs/Articles/2021/12/15/blog-global-debt-reaches-a-record-226-trillion

p. 7   'In the US, government debt . . . reached 97 per cent only a few years after the crisis, in 2012': https://fred.stlouisfed.org/series/GFDEGDQ188S

p. 7   'Meanwhile, the combined global debt levels of governments, businesses and individuals exceeded 250 per cent of GDP, reaching a total of $226 trillion': https://www.imf.org/en/Blogs/Articles/2021/12/15/blog-global-debt-reaches-a-record-226-trillion

Notes

1. THE SAVING MYTH

p. 18 'in the US and most other Western economies, from the post-war era until 2008 . . . the rate of interest you could expect to earn on your savings was higher than the rate of inflation': https://www.longtermtrends.net/real-interest-rate/

p. 19 'In the UK and Eurozone, inflation reached double digits': https://www.bankofengland.co.uk/explainers/will-inflation-in-the-uk-keep-rising; https://www.euronews.com/business/2024/03/05/inflation-in-europe-which-countries-have-the-highest-and-lowest-inflation-rates

p. 19 'in the US it peaked at 9.1 per cent': https://www.whitehouse.gov/cea/written-materials/2024/07/11/inflation-cools-in-2024q2/

p. 20 '$20 trillion of that debt . . . has been accumulated in the last fifteen years alone': https://fred.stlouisfed.org/series/GFDEBTN

p. 20 'In 2001, the US was paying an average interest rate of 6.5 per cent on its debt; by 2020 this had fallen to 2.4 per cent': https://fiscaldata.treasury.gov/datasets/average-interest-rates-treasury-securities/average-interest-rates-on-u-s-treasury-securities

p. 20 'Debt as a proportion of GDP rose from 55 per cent to 123 per cent': https://fiscaldata.treasury.gov/americas-finance-guide/national-debt/

p. 21 'Between 2022 and 2023 alone, US government debt increased by half a trillion dollars': https://fred.stlouisfed.org/series/GFDEBTN

p. 21 'at the time of writing, 39 cents of every dollar of income tax paid in the US is being used purely to pay interest on the debt': https://www.crfb.org/blogs/interest-rates-surge-near-record-highs

Notes

p. 22   'In 2022, the Governor of the Bank of England suggested that workers should exercise "restraint" in asking for pay rises for precisely this reason': https://www.theguardian.com/business/2022/feb/04/bank-of-england-boss-calls-for-wage-restraint-to-help-control-inflation

p. 26   'the UK's Office for National Statistics reports that housing, food, healthcare, insurance and transportation combined makes up 72 per cent of the average family's total expenditure': https://www.ons.gov.uk/peoplepopulationandcommunity/personalandhouseholdfinances/expenditure/bulletins/familyspendingintheuk/april2022tomarch2023

p. 26   'In the US, the Bureau of Labor Statistics calculates that the figure is closer to 82.5 per cent': https://www.bls.gov/news.release/cesan.nr0.htm

2. THE EARLY RETIREMENT MYTH

p. 39   '"To be honest, there's only so much relaxing you can do. I'm only young and a bit of hard work never did anyone any harm"': http://news.bbc.co.uk/1/hi/wales/south_east/7311542.stm

p. 39   '"more hours into the business than I ever did working before"': https://www.thenorthernecho.co.uk/news/6972649.millionaires-next-door/

p. 39   '"I gave up work for fourteen years, but I got bored. I started a sheet metal business, and I'm fitter and happier than I've been for years"': https://www.lottery24.com/news/lottery-millionaire-back-to-work

p. 39   'a third of lottery jackpot winners set up their own business, and almost the same amount again go back to life as an employee': https://www.theguardian.com/money/2005/mar/07/careers.theguardian4

177

Notes

p. 40 '"Now I'm living the Early Retirement dream. Guess what? I find myself fantasising about returning to work"': https://sexhealthmoneydeath.com/2016/02/03/fantasy-job/

p. 40 'data from rural China': https://www.sciencedaily.com/releases/2019/10/191029131506.htm

p. 41 'Retirement . . . often leads to losses "of income, purpose or, most poignantly, relevance"': https://www.economist.com/business/2024/01/25/why-you-should-never-retire

p. 41 'a study of Millennial Americans put the ideal retirement age at sixty-one': https://www.bankrate.com/personal-finance/smart-money/financial-milestones-survey-july-2018/

p. 42 'In 1930, 58 per cent of men over sixty-five were still working; by the year 2000 that number had fallen to 17.5 per cent': https://eh.net/encyclopedia/economic-history-of-retirement-in-the-united-states/

p. 42 'whereas now he might have another twenty': https://www.ssa.gov/oact/TR/2011/lr5a4.html

p. 42 'In the UK, the most common age of death for a woman is now eighty-nine': https://www.ons.gov.uk/peoplepopulationandcommunity/birthsdeathsandmarriages/lifeexpectancies/articles/mortalityinenglandandwales/pastandprojectedtrendsinaveragelifespan

p. 43 'By 2013, this had fallen to 2.8': https://www.ssa.gov/history/ratios.html#:~:text=Year

p. 47 'Rachel Accurso . . . has 7 million subscribers and is estimated to earn up to $15 million per year': https://www.dailymail.co.uk/femail/article-13833971/ms-rachel-miscarriage-songson.html

p. 47 'a series of study guides that now generates more than a million dollars per year': https://www.youtube.com/watch?v=6xJrJ4-p5Og

p. 49 'academics in Germany followed more than 700 people from the point of graduation, and found that high self-efficacy

Notes

translated into better pay and higher work satisfaction seven years later': ttps://www.sciencedirect.com/science/article/abs/pii/S0001879108000973

p. 50 'according to a global report on the link between skills and earnings, IT professionals who earn a new certification can increase their salary by $12,000 or more': https://www.forbes.com/sites/louiscolumbus/2020/11/14/which-tech-certifications-and-expertise-pay-the-most-this-year/

p. 50 'The Project Management Institute . . . found that those with a project management qualification earn 22 per cent more than those who lack one': https://www.pmi.org/learning/library/2020-salary-survey-11883

p. 50 'a study from the University of California found that people who demonstrated leadership skills early in life earned up to 33 per cent more as adults, even after controlling for differences in intelligence and other traits': https://www.journals.uchicago.edu/doi/abs/10.1086/430282?journalCode=jole

p. 50 'a study of more than 42,000 people by TalentSmart found that employees with high emotional intelligence (EQ) earned an average of $29,000 more per year than those with low EQ': https://www.talentsmarteq.com/increasing-your-salary-with-emotional-intelligence/

p. 51 'data from the US Bureau of Labor Statistics shows that journalists earn a median wage of $49,300': https://www.bls.gov/oes/2020/may/oes273023.htm

p. 51 'whereas for public relations specialists it's $66,750': https://www.bls.gov/ooh/media-and-communication/public-relations-specialists.htm

p. 51 'An analysis of 18 million employment records by Yahoo Money found that job switchers routinely increased their pay by significantly more than those who stayed put': https://money.yahoo.com/job-switchers-are-the-big-winners-202624616.html?guccounter=1

Notes

p. 53   'Rand knew his value: he demanded a fee of $100,000': https://www.amazon.co.uk/Steve-Jobs-Exclusive-Walter-Isaacson/dp/034914043X

p. 57   'She's now estimated to be making more than $200,000 per year': https://growthinreverse.com/rachel-karten/

p. 57   'Two years later, he packaged up this knowledge into a course that people can buy online': https://www.benlcollins.com/about/

3. THE RISK-MINIMISATION MYTH

p. 63   'Chhabra was an executive at the investment bank Merrill Lynch, and would go on to manage the money of one of the world's most successful investors and biggest philanthropists': https://pitchbook.com/profiles/limited-partner/170837-92#overview

p. 64   'Markowitz . . . used all manner of fancy maths to work out how an investor should maximise their return without taking on an unacceptable amount of risk': https://onlinelibrary.wiley.com/doi/abs/10.1111/j.1540-6261.1952.tb01525.x

p. 66   'Chhabra's write-up of his research has been cited in later academic papers fewer than a thousand times': https://papers.ssrn.com/sol3/papers.cfm?abstract_id=925138

p. 66   'compared to Markowitz's 66,000 (and Nobel medal)': https://papers.ssrn.com/sol3/papers.cfm?abstract_id=925138

p. 66   'From 1972 until 2019, an investor in a 60/40 mix of global stocks and bonds would have enjoyed an average annual return of 7.5 per cent, with a standard deviation . . . of 10.3 per cent': Historic returns calculated from historical data using portfoliovisualizer.com.

p. 67   'From 2020 until mid-2024, the average return from the same portfolio fell to 5.1 per cent while volatility increased to 14 per

Notes

cent': Historic returns calculated from historical data using portfoliovisualizer.com

p. 69 'The American journalist H. L. Mencken once quipped that a wealthy man is one who earns $100 a year more than his wife's sister's husband': https://www.goodreads.com/quotes/8220513-a-wealthy-man-is-one-who-earns-100-a-year

p. 69 '"Social comparison theory" . . . describes the fact that poor people can be happier than wealthy people if they're relatively well-off by the standards of their surroundings': https://journals.sagepub.com/doi/10.1177/001872675400700202

p. 69 'Michael Kraus and Jacinth Tan replicated this finding by analysing studies with a total of 2.3 million participants': https://ink.library.smu.edu.sg/soss_research/3244/

p. 70 'In 2014, the pair introduced what they call the "generalised friendship paradox"': https://arxiv.org/abs/1401.1458

p. 73 'This phenomenon . . . was famously demonstrated by the behavioural economists Amos Tversky and Daniel Kahneman in the 1990s, and is often used to demonstrate that humans are irrational and subject to biases when it comes to investing': https://www.jstor.org/stable/2937956

4. THE HOME-OWNERSHIP MYTH

p. 82 'Noah Kagan': https://noahkagan.com/investment-thesis/

p. 82 'Shaan Puri': https://www.youtube.com/watch?v=liRUa-Q5hF8&t=595s

p. 85 'In the UK, where owner-occupiers stay in the same home for an average of nearly seventeen years, 30 per cent of homes have two or more spare bedrooms': https://www.gov.uk/government/statistics/chapters-for-english-housing-survey-2022-to-2023-headline-report/chapter-3-housing-history-and-future-housing

Notes

p. 88 'according to an analysis by *The Economist*, it's cheaper to rent than to own in 89 per cent of US counties': https://www.economist.com/united-states/2023/11/30/is-it-cheaper-to-rent-or-buy-property

p. 88 'In the UK, only 54 per cent of renters have any level of savings, compared to 71 per cent of those who own with a mortgage and 86 per cent of those who own outright': https://www.nimblefins.co.uk/savings-accounts/average-household-savings-uk#home

p. 88 'meanwhile, the median net worth of the typical US renter is $6,300, while the median net worth of the typical US homeowner is $255,000': https://www.federalreserve.gov/publications/files/scf20.pdf

p. 89 'If you'd bought a house in the US in 1890, twenty-five years later it would have increased in value by less than the rate of inflation': https://www.longtermtrends.net/home-price-vs-inflation/

p. 90 'a typical family home that would have cost $23,000 in 1970 was worth $130,000 by 1995': https://fred.stlouisfed.org/series/MSPUS

p. 90 'Between 1995 and 2020, they increased by an astonishing 116 per cent': https://www.nationwidehousepriceindex.co.uk/resources/f/uk-data-series

p. 90 'As we entered the 1990s, the US interest rate was 8.25 per cent. By the time we entered the 2000s, it was 5.5 per cent. By the time we entered the 2010s, it was at 0.25 per cent': https://fred.stlouisfed.org/series/FEDFUNDS

p. 90 'The pattern in the UK was the same: indeed, in the early 1990s rates briefly spiked up to 15 per cent. By the turn of the millennium, they'd fallen to 5.5 per cent, and by 2020 had reached an all-time low of 0.1 per cent': https://www.bankofengland.co.uk/boeapps/database/Bank-Rate.asp

Notes

p. 91 'But the nominal price – the price they could expect to sell it for – increased by 391 per cent': https://www.nationwidehousepriceindex.co.uk/resources/f/uk-data-series

p. 92 'an asset that typically rises in value at least along with inflation over the long term': https://blogs.lse.ac.uk/usappblog/2020/03/09/over-150-years-of-data-show-that-trends-in-uk-and-us-house-prices-have-little-in-common/

5. THE COMPOUNDING MYTH

p. 98 'Popular investment platform Nutmeg refers to it as a "miracle"': https://www.nutmeg.com/nutmegonomics/the-extraordinary-power-of-compound-returns

p. 98 'ski-slope of doom': https://www.lcp.com/media/1150069/the-ski-slope-of-doom-is-this-the-most-worrying-chart-in-pensions.pdf

p. 98 'slow-motion car crash': https://www.pensionsage.com/pa/Direction-of-pensions-a-slow-motion-car-crash-Webb.php

p. 99 'what the Pension and Lifetime Savings Association defines as a "comfortable" retirement income of £43,100': https://www.retirementlivingstandards.org.uk/details

p. 99 'Plugging this into a retirement calculator reveals that for someone in the UK who qualifies for the full level of state support, this would require a pension pot of more than £650,000': https://www.nutsaboutmoney.com/pensions/retirement-income-calculator?pension-pot=650000#moderate

p. 102 'stock markets tend to crash (defined as a decline of more than 30 per cent) once every twelve years': https://awealthofcommonsense.com/2022/01/how-often-should-you-expect-a-stock-market-correction/

p. 104 'This is why Warren Buffett made 99 per cent of his wealth after he turned sixty-five': https://www.cnbc.com/2024/05/

Notes

03/most-of-warren-buffetts-wealth-came-after-age-65-heres-why.html

p. 108 '"the first rule of compounding is not to interrupt it unnecessarily"': https://www.forbes.com/sites/andrewrosen/2024/03/21/investment-advice-from-investing-legend-charlie-munger/

p. 108 'A popular online brokerage set out to identify what set their top performing clients apart from the rest, and discovered that they had an unexpected edge: they were dead': https://www.fool.co.uk/2016/10/31/the-best-investors-are-dead/

6. THE DIVERSIFICATION MYTH

p. 115 'those holding 100 per cent of their investment in stocks . . . saw their portfolios drop in value by 6 per cent': https://www.vanguardinvestor.co.uk/investments/vanguard-lifestrategy-100-equity-fund-accumulation-shares/price-performance

p. 115 'their investments ended the year down by more than 11 per cent': https://www.vanguardinvestor.co.uk/investments/vanguard-lifestrategy-60-equity-fund-accumulation-shares/price-performance

p. 117 'the loss of nearly 20 per cent that you'd have experienced by Christmas': https://uk.finance.yahoo.com/quote/SPY/history/?period1=1640995200&period2=1672444800

p. 118 'who watched in frustration as it took sixteen years to beat the level it achieved on the last day of the twentieth century': https://uk.finance.yahoo.com/quote/%5EFTSE/

p. 119 'Between 2013 and 2023, more than $100 trillion of extra debt was issued globally': https://www.reuters.com/business/global-debt-hits-new-record-high-313-trillion-iif-2024-02-21/

p. 120 'the long-term return on bonds has been around 6 per cent per year – compared with 10 per cent for the stock market':

Notes

https://money.cnn.com/retirement/guide/investing_bonds.moneymag/index3.htm

p. 122 'According to market data service Morningstar, bond volatility more than doubled in the years 2022–2023 compared to the preceding seven years': https://www.morningstar.co.uk/uk/news/244975/why-have-bonds-been-so-volatile.aspx

p. 122 '2022 was the first time in history that the US stock and bond markets had both fallen by double-digit percentages': https://www.marketwatch.com/story/2022-was-the-biggest-outlier-year-in-markets-history-as-stocks-and-bonds-both-plunged-deutsche-bank-says-11672859958

p. 122 'Having been sitting at a correlation level of -0.6 pre-pandemic (only fractionally off an all-time low), they soared to a positive level of 0.6': https://www.morningstar.co.uk/uk/news/244975/why-have-bonds-been-so-volatile.aspx

p. 126 'you would at one point have experienced a peak-to-trough drop of 55 per cent': Historic returns calculated from historical data using portfoliovisualizer.com.

p. 128 'a house would have cost the same amount of gold in 1979 as it did in 2024': https://www.longtermtrends.net/real-estate-gold-ratio/

p. 128 'over shorter periods its record is less consistent': https://www.forbes.com/advisor/investing/gold-inflation-hedge/

p. 129 'Morris' BOLD index . . . has, since 2015, dramatically outperformed even the best-performing stock markets . . . with surprisingly low volatility': https://bold.report/

p. 130 'as a pure investment there are thought to be 2.3 million holders of buy-to-let property in the UK': https://www.gov.uk/government/publications/a-fairer-private-rented-sector/a-fairer-private-rented-sector

p. 130 'and there are an estimated 19.3 million rental homes in the US': https://www.bankrate.com/mortgages/investment-property-statistics/

Notes

p. 130 'The data here only goes back to 1994, but since then this particular allocation would have achieved an annual return of 7.44 per cent': Historic returns calculated from historical data using portfoliovisualizer.com

7. THE 'TOO RISKY' MYTH

p. 140 'Google searches for "manifesting" have more than doubled since 2020': https://trends.google.com/trends/explore?date=today%205-y&q=manifesting&hl=en-GB

p. 140 '"The super-rich did not earn their wealth by building conventional portfolios based on the principles of asset allocation and diversification. In fact, they did just the opposite"': https://www.amazon.co.uk/Aspirational-Investor-Taming-Markets-Achieve/dp/0062235095

p. 144 'Given that property growth in the US and UK has historically outpaced inflation': https://journals.sagepub.com/doi/abs/10.1177/0042098019872691?journalCode=usja

p. 144 'the inflation figure itself has averaged more than the 2 per cent target since it was first adopted': https://www.in2013dollars.com/uk/inflation/2003?amount=100

p. 146 'If you'd bought shares in payment processing company Square in 2019, you would have paid around $70 for them – and been delighted when you'd virtually tripled your money two years later': https://uk.finance.yahoo.com/quote/SQ/

p. 146 'you'd have been horrified to watch their share price plunge from £150 to mere pennies in the same timeframe': https://uk.finance.yahoo.com/quote/0O8X.IL/

p. 149 'putting $500,000 into Facebook in its early days, which became more than a billion dollars when he sold after the company went public': https://money.cnn.com/2012/08/20/technology/facebook-peter-thiel/index.html

INDEX

Accurso, Rachel, 47
Adams, Douglas, 155
Amazon, 118
angel investments, 149–50
Apple, 53, 118, 119–20
Australia, 79, 145
Automatic Millionaire, The (Bach), 18

Bach, David, 18
base rate, 22
billionaires *see* wealth
Binghamton University, New York, 40
bitcoin, 129
Bogle, John C., 97–8
Bogleheads' Guide to Investing, The (Lindauer, LeBoeuf, Larimore), 137
BOLD index, 129
bonds, 115, 119–26, 133, 141
    volatility of, 122–3
BrewDog, 150
Browne, Harry, 125–30
Brudenell, Mark, 39
budgeting, 26–7
Buffett, Warren, 104, 108
Bureau of Labour Statistics (US), 26, 51
businesses, 148–50
    business development, 55

Canada, 79, 145
Candy, Christian and Nick, 141
careers *see* employment
Carnegie, Dale, 17
cash, 80–84, 126–7, 131
central banks, 6–7, 22–3
Chhabra, Ashvin, 63–6, 69, 133, 140
China, 40–41
Clason, George S., 17
Collins, Ben, 57
'compounding returns', 10, 97–111
    automation and, 108–9, 110–11
    difficulty of, 106–7
    limitations of, 102–4
consultants, 53–5
Covid-19 pandemic, 19, 22–3, 121, 127
crowdfunding platforms, 150

debt, 142–5
Dominguez, Joe, 98
Dumoulin, James, 137, 148

earning, 35, 44–58, 161–2
    'impact equation', 46–7, 52
    see also employment
Economist, The, 41, 88
Einstein, Albert, 98
emergency funds, 71, 75, 80–83, 157
emotional intelligence (EQ), 50

Index

employment, 44–58
    career self-efficacy, 49–50
    contract work, 53–5
    job switching, 51–2
    re-framing your career, 49–50
    skills and qualifications, 50–51
    see also earning
energy, cost of, 23
Eom, Young-Ho, 70
Eurozone, 7, 19, 21
Exchange Traded Funds (ETFs), 76, 132

Facebook, 149
'Fed Funds rate' *see* 'base rate'
Federal Reserve, 5–6, 17, 20
Festinger, Leon, 69
finance influencers, 101, 140
financial crisis (2007–2008), 6–7, 127
financial independence, 48–58, 155–73
FIRE (Financial Independence, Retire Early), 40, 44
France, 41
'free money' era, 7–8, 21, 67, 101, 145
friendship, 70
FTSE 100, 116, 118

GameStop, 146
GDP, 23
'generalised friendship paradox', 70
Germany, 49, 79
Gibney, Roy, 39
gold, investment in, 126, 128–9
gold standard, 5–7
government debt, 7, 9, 20–21, 127
Graham, Benjamin, 121
Gross, Bill, 141

home ownership, 75, 79–94, 157–8
    deposits, 93
    house prices, 89–92, 142–3
    mortgages, 43, 84–8, 91–2, 142, 144–5
    renting and, 87–9, 92–4
    see also property investment
How to Win Friends and Influence People (Carnegie), 17
hyperinflation, 23

index funds, 116–19, 132, 146
inequality, 5
inflation, 8–9, 18–24, 81, 100, 102, 123, 128–9
    house prices and, 91
    hyperinflation, 23
    'inflationary spiral', 22
Inflation-Proofing Your Investments (Browne), 125–6
Intelligent Investor, The (Graham), 121
interest rates, 6–8, 18–24, 81, 101
    'base rate', 22
    house prices and, 90–91, 145
    'real' interest rate, 20
investments, 32, 34–5, 63–76, 97–111, 147, 157–60
    age and, 72–3
    angel investments, 149–50
    bonds, 115, 119–26, 133
    businesses, 148–50
    'compounding returns', 10, 97–111, 160–61
    diversification, 115–33, 137, 140–41, 147–8, 157, 159–60
    focus and, 140–42
    gold, 126, 128–9

Index

improving financial status, 69–75, 158–60, 162–3
index funds, 116–19, 146
loss aversion, 73–4
maintaining your lifestyle, 68–9, 71–5, 105–6, 158–60
property, 92, 129–31, 143–6
protection against disaster, 68, 71–5, 80–84, 156–7, 158–60
risk (volatility) and, 63–8, 72–4, 137–51
shares, 71, 89, 117, 123, 143, 146–8
stocks, 115–16, 121–6, 132–3, 160
iShares world tracker, 118

Jo, Hang-Hyun, 70
Jobs, Steve, 53

Kagan, Noah, 82
Kahneman, Daniel, 73
Karten, Rachel, 56–7
Kraus, Michael, 69

Larimore, Taylor, 137
LeBoeuf, Michael, 137
leverage, 142–5
Libertarian Party (US), 125
'life extensionists', 12
lifestyle, 68–9, 70
    upgrading, 138–9
Linares, Mike, 47
Lindauer, Mel, 137
Link in Bio (newsletter), 57
Little Book of Common Sense Investing, The (Bogle), 97–8
loss aversion, 73–4
lottery winners, 39

Malkiel, Burton G., 115
Markowitz, Harry, 64–6, 121
Mencken, H. L., 69
Merrill Lynch investment bank, 63
Meta, 118
Microsoft, 118
Millionaire Next Door, The (Stanley), 137
millionaires *see* wealth
Modern Portfolio Theory, 76, 121
Monzo, 150
Morningstar (market data service), 122
Morris, Charlie, 129
mortgages, 43, 84–8, 91–2
Munger, Charlie, 108

Nasdaq, 129
Netherlands, 79
New Zealand, 79
NeXT (technology company), 53
Nixon, Richard, 6
Nutmeg (investment platform), 98
Nvidia, 116, 118

Oculus, 150
Office for National Statistics (UK), 26
'overemployed' community, 45

'pay yourself first' concept, 32–3, 109
'penny stocks', 139
Pension and Lifetime Savings Association, 99
pensions, 98–100, 109–10, 158
    pension age, 41
    state pension, 42
    see also retirement

Index

'Permanent Portfolio', 125–30, 132
PIMCO (Pacific Investment Management Company), 141
Pittard, Luke, 39
politics, 127
private equity, 149
Project Management Institute, 50
property investment, 92, 129–31, 143–6
Property Podcast, The, 10, 79
Puri, Shaan, 82

Ramsey, Dave, 18
Rand, Paul, 53
Random Walk Down Wall Street, A (Malkiel), 115
Real Estate Investment Trusts (REITs), 130
recessions, 126–7
Reddit, 45
rental market, 87–9, 92–4, 144–5
retirement, 4, 10, 39–59, 68, 86, 98–100
    early retirement, 39–40, 44
    lifespan and, 42, 44
    see also pensions
Richest Man in Babylon, The (Clason), 17–18, 71
risk *see* investments
Robin, Vicki, 98

S&P 500, 129
savings, 10, 17–35
    emergency funds, 71, 75, 80–83, 157
    income and, 33–4
    inflation and, 18–24
    interest rates and, 19–24
    'pay yourself first' concept, 32–3, 109
    spending, 24–33
self-help books, 17–18
shares, 71, 89, 117, 123, 143, 146–8
share prices, 89
Sheeran, Ed, 46
Silbert, Barry, 141
'social comparison theory', 69
social media, 4–5, 101, 140
Social Security Act (US, 1935), 42
specialist knowledge, 146–8
spending, 24–33, 156
    audits, 29–30
    budgeting and, 26–7
    fixed costs, 30–31
    'mindful spending', 25–32, 156
    'pay yourself first' concept, 32–3
    tracking, 27–8
    'two-week rule', 28–9
Square (payment processing company), 146
Stanley, Thomas J., 137
state pension, 42
stock market, 13
stocks, 115–16, 121–6, 132–3
    volatility of, 122–3

TalentSmart, 50
Tan, Jacinth, 69
Thiel, Peter, 149
Total Money Makeover, The (Ramsey), 18
Tversky, Amos, 73

United States, 26, 79
    bonds, 120, 122
    gold standard and, 5–6
    government debt, 7, 9, 20–22
    housing, 88, 89–90, 130, 144–5

Index

inflation and, 19, 23
interest rates, 6–7, 18, 90
retirement, 41, 42
stock market, 101, 116, 118–19, 122, 139
taxation, 17
workforce, 4, 51
universities, 4, 48
University of California, 50

Vanguard (investment platform), 115

wealth, 66, 70, 72, 82, 137–45, 148, 150–51
WeWork, 116
Wirecard (payment processing company), 146
work *see* employment
wtfhappenedin1971.com, 4–5

Yahoo Money, 51
Your Money or Your Life (Robin, Dominguez), 98
YouTube, 47, 148

ABOUT THE AUTHOR

Rob Dix started investing as a hobby using his spare cash, but soon became obsessed. Over the next ten years, he would do everything he could to educate himself about the financial world and to pass on what he learned.

Today, Rob is one of Britain's best-respected finance experts. Whether he's presenting *The Property Podcast* (Britain's most-downloaded investment podcast) or writing his weekly property column for the *Sunday Times*, Rob is on a mission to teach the world about how money, the economy and investment really work.

Rob's most recent book, *The Price of Money*, was an instant *Sunday Times* bestseller that revealed what has gone wrong in the global economy over the last decade. Now, Rob reveals what this new financial era means for anyone who wants to build lasting wealth.

NOW CLAIM YOUR FREE BONUSES

Congratulations on finishing the book! But let's be honest: reading alone won't change your financial life. The real work starts now.

To help you put these ideas into action, I've created some free bonus resources:

- **Video course:** I'll walk you through the book's key concepts and share extra tips to get you started.

- **Digital workbook:** Plan your path to financial freedom, with targeted advice to overcome common hurdles.

- **One-page cheat sheet:** All the essential takeaways at your fingertips, ready to print and reference anytime.

Ready to make some changes? Head to **robdix.com/myths** to claim your bonuses, and I'll email everything straight to your inbox.